Drug War Addiction

Notes from the Front Lines of America's #1 Policy Disaster

by Sheriff Bill Masters
libertybill.net

Accurate Press
St. Louis, Missouri

Drug War Addiction
Notes from the Front Lines of America's #1 Policy Disaster

©2001 by Bill Masters

ISBN 1-888118-09-1 paperback $10.95
Printed in the United States of America

Published by Accurate Press, a division of
Accuprint, Inc.
P.O. Box 86
Lonedell, MO 63060 U.S.A.
http://www.accuratepress.net
1-800-374-4049

Dedicated to the American peace officer.

Acknowledgements

In this book, I share some of my experiences as a law enforcement officer who has spent two decades dealing with the war on drugs. I'd like to thank a number of people for helping me with the project. My wife Jill has offered her support and encouragement through the years. Richard Lamping was instrumental in getting this project off the ground, and Dawn Lamping helped to edit the text. Ari Armstrong also helped with the editing process and he helped me research a variety of issues. Jennifer Armstrong provided her expertise in graphic design. Fred Boucher assisted with the copy editing. I especially want to thank the men and women in law enforcement I've worked with over the years to keep violent criminals off the streets.

Contents

Introduction
The Drug War As Addiction

THE SO-CALLED "WAR ON DRUGS" is itself an addiction.

It's an addiction more harmful to the fabric of American society than drug use could ever be.

The Random House dictionary defines "addicted" as "devoted or given up to a practice or habit or to something habit-forming." That describes the war on drugs to a T.

The first way the drug war has become an addiction is obvious: law enforcement agencies are addicted to the money. Billions of dollars are spent in an effort to stop the flow of drugs into and around this country. Many thousands of jobs are tied directly to drug interdiction. Some communities have become dependent on prisons for their economic survival, prisons which warehouse the hundreds of thousands of non-violent drug offenders. The federal government gives money to state and local governments to enforce drug laws. Police forces everywhere use the money to pay for more personnel, more machine guns, and more high-tech surveillance equipment. Police also confiscate property—cars, boats, houses, cash—and keep the proceeds, often without even filing criminal charges. Even the military is involved. U.S. troops fight the drug war both at home and abroad.

Sheriff Bill Masters

The other ways the drug war has become an addiction are not so obvious, though they're even more important. The public has become addicted to the belief that government should use force to make people act responsibly in their personal lives. True, a lot of people in this country have a drug problem, whether that problem is with cocaine, heroin, or alcohol. That's a problem for friends, counselors, parents, and spiritual leaders to address. Instead of dealing with the problem, we want to "pass the buck" to armed police agents.

When people buy into propaganda campaigns and corresponding government programs, they avoid taking personal responsibility for helping those in need. In the 1910s, prohibitionists argued taking a drink would damage your heart and make you go crazy. (Today, many doctors think moderate drinking helps your heart.) Later, the propaganda turned to "reefer madness." At various times, drug prohibition has been perpetuated by racism, whether against Blacks, Hispanics, or Asians. Some people want to believe drugs are akin to demonic possession, so they can support prohibition and wash their hands of the problem, as if the problem will just disappear once we throw enough dollars and firepower at it. A lot of times drugs are called "dope" because they can make you stupid. Some of the most widely distributed "dope" in America is drug war propaganda.

But perhaps the most lazy drug war addicts are our political leaders. Politicians who don't want to make any real changes in the way government works peddle fear among the electorate and claim they'll "get tough on crime." This is a great gimmick, because the "tougher" politicians get on drug dealers, the more profitable drug dealing becomes. It's a reinforcing loop, a downward spiral. Through prohibition, politicians increase their budgets, their staff, and their power. Unfortunately, power-hungry politicians and gullible voters are trapped in a damaging codependent relationship.

Our country has been mainlining the drug war for decades. As with all addictions, believing is habit-forming. "It's not hurting me." Have you ever looked at the difference in violent crime rates between the inner cities and the rest of America? Have you checked out the number of minorities rotting in prison? The increased potency and impurity of drugs? The amount and depth of police corruption? The ludicrous expense of prohibition? The endless loss of individual rights in the name of the drug war? When reformers point to the flaws and problems of the drug war, the warriors' answer is to do more of it. More money. More guns. More authoritarian control. Isn't that the response of all addicts?

The first step to curing any addiction is to admit we have a problem. The drug war doesn't work. It doesn't keep people from ruining their lives with drugs. If anything, prohibition makes it harder for people to seek treatment. And along the way all of us suffer the loss of our privacy, our safety, our money, and our rights as Americans.

> "These (drug enforcement) agencies are all addicted to the funding."
>
> —Orange County Superior Court Judge James P. Gray Denver's KOA 850AM, May 22, 2001

Recovery will be a long and difficult process. Before we get better, our country will suffer withdrawal pains. Just as an individual addict experiences conflicting emotions and relapses, so our nation will see die-hard drug warriors and prohibitionists fight the reformers at every turn. But once we get serious about curing our drug war addiction, we can also get serious about truly helping people with real problems.

Chapter 1
Remember Zeke: "Collateral Damage" in the War on Drugs

BEFORE OKLAHOMA CITY BOMBER Timothy McVeigh was executed, he said the children he murdered were "collateral damage." The press and the public were rightfully outraged. Yet when innocent children, mothers, and fathers are killed in the drug war, a lot of people shrug their shoulders and accept those deaths as the costs of waging the war.

Of course, the phrase "drug war" is just a euphemism. You can't wage war on plants and household chemicals. You can only wage war against other people. The war on drugs is really a war on drug addicts, families, casual drug users, and totally innocent people. The rhetoric of the "drug war" was invoked precisely to create the type of wartime hysteria among the populace that leads people to patriotically follow their leaders into battle, and to make deep personal sacrifices for the sake of war. As Randolph Bourne wrote in the early 1900s:

War is the health of the State. It automatically sets in motion throughout society those irresistible forces for uniformity, for passionate cooperation with the Government in coercing into obedience the minority groups and individuals which lack the larger herd sense. The machinery of government sets and enforces the drastic penalties; the minorities are... intimidated into silence... [I]n general, the nation in wartime attains a uniformity of feeling, a hierarchy of values culminating at the undisputed apex of the State ideal, which could not possibly be produced through any other agency than war.

(http://www.slip.net/~knabb/CF/bourne.htm)

It is no coincidence that the military coined the phrase "collateral damage" to describe innocent deaths, and that the deaths caused by the war on drugs are generally viewed as "collateral damage."

Esequiel Hernandez

Zeke Hernandez' family members are proud Americans. They have a small ranch along the Rio Grande bordering Mexico, near the Texas town of Redford, population 100. The land there is poor, dry, mostly overgrown desert foliage and weeds. Zeke was a sophomore at the local high school, probably not going to Harvard, but known as a nice boy and well-liked by his classmates.

Esequiel Hernandez

Zeke liked to raise goats on his father's ranch. He enjoyed the responsibility, like many his age, of caring for the animals. Every day, after school, he took the goats out of their pens and herded them on the ranch, allowing them to forage on the scrub desert plants that only a goat would enjoy.

Years ago, Zeke was given an antique .22 caliber rifle by his grandfather. When herding his goats, he always took the little .22 with him to do some plinking and fend off the coyotes or wild dogs that would prey upon the goats.

But on this day, Zeke didn't see four U.S. Marines assigned to the "Joint Task Force Six" drug interdiction team. The plinking Zeke and his goats stumbled into the camouflaged Marines' ambush formation. The Marines, doing nothing more than what they are trained to do, without warning, shot and killed Zeke, thereby eliminating an armed threat to their mission of policing United States soil.

> "The wars that governments wage often kill far more bystanders than enemies. A sterling case in point is the...War on Drugs, which has destroyed lives, wasted billions of dollars, [and] besmirched the U.S. Constitution..."
>
> —James T. Bennett and Thomas DiLorenzo
> Official Lies, page 237

Donald Scott, age 62, was a wealthy man. He lived on a beautiful 250-acre ranch in California that bordered a federal park. The feds wanted to buy his ranch to include in the park, but Mr. Scott was not interested in selling. Federal agents flew over the house and claimed they saw marijuana growing on the property. They obtained a search warrant for the ranch.

In the early morning hours of the next day, a pounding on the door of their home awakened Mr. Scott and his wife Frances. When

Mrs. Scott attempted to open the door, a group of narcotics task force deputies burst into the house with guns in their hands. Mrs. Scott was pushed forcefully to the ground, a gun aimed at her head. She pleaded, "Please don't shoot me!" Hearing his wife's pleas, Mr. Scott armed himself with a revolver and ran out of his bedroom, only to be shot and killed instantly by the raiding officers. No marijuana plants or drugs of any kind were found on the Scott property.

Sixty-nine year old Ralph Garrison of New Mexico was awakened before sunrise one morning after hearing someone trying to break into the rental house next door that he owned. Knowing his tenants were out of town, he went outside to investigate. He saw a group of armed men on his property wearing dark clothing and black masks. He returned to his house and called 911. According to the reporters who listened to those 911 tapes, Mr. Garrison's voice was filled with "fear and panic."

Garrison then armed himself with a pistol and a cell phone and went to his back door to wait for the police to arrive. Three members of a police SWAT team who were busy breaking down the door of Mr. Garrison's unoccupied rental house immediately shot 12 rounds from their AR-15 assault rifles into Mr. Garrison as he stood in his own doorway. He was killed instantly.

Police in Texas were using a paid informant to buy $30 worth of drugs. The informant claimed he had purchased drugs at Annie Rae Dixon's house. The police raided the home, then shot and killed the 84-year-old, bedridden Mrs. Dixon. No illegal drugs were found in her home.

Ismael Mena from Mexico, father of nine, came to the United States legally for work to support his family. He worked the night shift at the Coca-Cola bottling plant. He was in his bedroom sleeping during the day when the Denver police department SWAT team raided his apartment after obtaining a "no-knock" search warrant for drugs. Mr. Mena, awakened by the black-clothed officers breaking down his door, armed himself with a .22 caliber pistol. Officers stormed into his bedroom and ordered him to drop the pistol. He started to drop the pistol; then, according to the SWAT team, he questioned, "Policia?" He was immediately shot in the head and chest, at which point, according to the officers, he reached for the gun again and in fact discharged the gun, but was shot six more times and killed. No illegal drugs were found in Mena's home.

Investigation revealed the police raided the wrong house. The narcotics officer in charge of the case, according to district attorney Dave Thomas, made false statements, knowing they were false, in order to obtain the search warrant. The officer was charged with three felonies, including perjury. However, he was allowed to plead guilty to a misdemeanor so he could retain his job as a police officer in Denver. He was recently given nine months of back pay, almost $40,000, and reinstated as a police officer for the city of Denver.

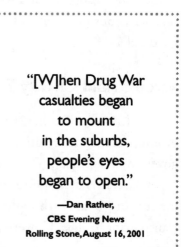

"[W]hen Drug War casualties began to mount in the suburbs, people's eyes began to open."

—Dan Rather,
CBS Evening News
Rolling Stone, August 16, 2001

Regarding the controversy over the officer's reinstatement, Denver mayor Wellington Webb stated, incredibly, "Mr. Mena would still be alive today if he just didn't have a gun."

The list of drug war victims goes on and on. I am talking about kids, old ladies, completely innocent people, shot and killed not by gangs, not by robbers or drug dealers, not by schoolyard shooters or kids playing with guns, but by those sworn to protect our lives.

One police bureaucrat said these shootings were "unintentional but not mistakes."

There is a reason why we are allowing these shootings to happen. We are in a war, a war on drugs. And during a time of war, innocent people get in the way sometimes. People's rights have to be placed on the back burner.

It is interesting to me that most people concerned about the erosion of the Second Amendment have all heard of Ruby Ridge and Waco, but because it was a "drug raid" we calmly accept the deaths of ranchers, businessmen, old ladies, children, and even innocent goatherders.

Veronica and Charity Bowers

Roni Bowers and her baby Charity were killed, but not by drug-dealing gangs or criminal thugs. Instead, they were killed by government agents.

A United States spotter aircraft, flying with a Peruvian air force officer on board, thought a civilian plane might have been transporting drugs. However, the only cargo was a human one of Baptist missionaries and their children, including seven-month-old Charity and her mother.

After spotting the civilian aircraft, the U.S. jet contacted the Peruvian air force, which then scrambled fighters to shoot at the helpless civilians.

A bullet ripped through Roni and into her baby, killing them both instantly. Witnessing this horror were Roni's husband, Jim, and their six-year-old son, Cory, who were passengers on the plane. During the attack the pilot of the civilian plane continued contact with civilian Peruvian air traffic controllers. According to press reports he said repeatedly, "They are killing us! They are killing us!"

After the plane was strafed, the American pilot working for the Baptist church was able to crash the burning plane into a river. The injured pilot, Jim, and young Cory were able to escape the wreckage and float down the river grasping dislodged pieces of aircraft. One fighter plane continued to shoot at them. Reuters reported that the U.S. plane watched the incident from about a mile away.

We shouldn't be surprised that this occurred. Mad as hell, maybe, but not surprised.

The increasing militarization of the drug war and our local police forces is a dangerous trend. Today most of the tactical and firearms training for "peace" officers comes straight out of military doctrine. The tactics taught are not of negotiations or individual bravery but of concentration of forces and firepower.

In Colorado, the legislature has passed laws requiring the Governor "as Commander in Chief" to use the soldiers of the Colorado National Guard for drug interdiction and enforcement.

> "As in any war, there is an ever-growing roster of innocent victims: people who have the bad fortune to run afoul of warriors pursuing their objective with crushing intensity, sometimes people simply in the wrong place at the wrong time."
>
> —Ted Galen Carpenter
> After Prohibition, page 147

To that end, the soldiers are providing "aviation assets and ground assistance units trained for the specific mission of cannabis suppression and eradication." They are available to local law enforcement in "narcotics-centered investigations with surveillance platforms, thermal imagery and night vision equipment, case support and intelligence analysis."

The soldiers are also training local officers at the County Sheriffs of Colorado facility in Douglas County on issues like "non-urban tactical operations" and "airmobile drug enforcement operations."

It is only a matter of time before our increasingly militarized tactics will result in more unintended deaths like those in Peru. I question whether it is worth it.

EVENTUALLY WE WILL REALIZE A FIST WON'T WORK
AGAINST WHAT IS FUNDAMENTALLY A SPIRITUAL PROBLEM.

Policing and blaming Peru, Columbia, or Mexico for our nation's drug problems is a little like blaming Saudi Arabia for traffic jams. This is a demand problem, not a supply problem.

We shut off the cocaine supply, then some people start cooking meth in their homes. We stop the meth and many will get high on ecstasy, booze, the doctor's pills or whatever. Controlling the drug supply is like holding water in a fist—it just leaks out and goes on to something else. Eventually we will realize a fist won't work against what is fundamentally a spiritual problem.

Before we suffer more innocent deaths at the hands of those sworn to protect us, before we lose touch with our local peace officers, and before more children overdose because we haven't identified or addressed the demand problem, we must rethink the drug war. We must change strategies.

Peter McWilliams

The drug war has claimed the lives of people who never had anything to do with drugs. Peter McWilliams did take drugs—he smoked marijuana to reduce his nausea. He was also a vocal opponent of drug prohibition. The Libertarian Party sent out the following press release June 17, 2000, about Peter McWilliams' death. Peter's books, including his best-selling *Ain't Nobody's Business If You Do*, are published at www.mcwilliams.com.

CALIFORNIA—Peter McWilliams, the #1 bestselling author and medical marijuana activist who was found dead in California on June 14, was murdered by the War on Drugs, the Libertarian Party charged.

"Peter McWilliams would not be dead today if not for the heartless, lethal War on Drugs," said Steve Dasbach, the party's national director. "The federal government killed Peter McWilliams by denying him the medical marijuana he needed to stay alive as surely as if its drug warriors had put a gun to his head and pulled the trigger.

"Peter McWilliams may be dead, but the causes he so bravely fought for—access to life-saving medicine, an end to the War on Drugs, and greater freedom for all Americans—will live on."

> "[M]any of our drug laws are scandalously draconian and the sentences are often savage... [T]he war on drugs has done considerable damage to the Fourth Amendment..."
>
> —Judge Morris S. Arnold
> **Why Our Drug Laws Have Failed, page 95**

On Wednesday, McWilliams was found dead in the bathroom of his Los Angeles home. According to sources, he had choked on his vomit.

McWilliams, 50, had suffered from AIDS and non-Hodgkin's lymphoma since 1996, and had used marijuana to suppress the nausea that was a common side effect to the potent medications needed to keep him alive.

The marijuana was completely legal, thanks to California's

Proposition 215, which passed in 1996 and legalized the use of marijuana for treatment of illness. However, in late 1997, McWilliams was arrested by federal drug agents and charged with conspiracy to sell marijuana.

After a federal judge ruled that McWilliams could not mention his illnesses at his trial—or introduce as evidence any of the documented benefits of medical marijuana—he pled guilty to avoid a 10-year mandatory-minimum prison sentence.

"A GOOD, DECENT, TALENTED MAN IS DEAD BECAUSE OF THE BIPARTISAN PUBLIC POLICY DISASTER KNOWN AS THE WAR ON DRUGS."

While out on bail awaiting sentencing, McWilliams was prohibited from using marijuana—and being denied access to the drug's anti-nausea properties almost certainly caused his death, said Dasbach.

"First, the federal government arrested McWilliams for doing something that is 100% legal in California," he said. "Then, they put him on trial and wouldn't allow him to introduce the one piece of evidence that could have explained his actions. Finally, they let him out of jail on the condition that he couldn't use the one medicine that kept him alive.

"What the federal government did to Peter McWilliams is nothing less than cold-blooded, premeditated murder. A good, decent, talented man is dead because of the bipartisan public policy disaster known as the War on Drugs."

Ironically, on June 9, McWilliams appeared on the "Give Me A Break!" segment of ABC Television's 20/20, where host John Stossel noted, "[McWilliams] is out of prison on the condition that he not smoke marijuana, but it was the marijuana that kept him from vomiting up his medication. I can understand that the federal drug police don't agree with what some states have decided to do about medical marijuana, but does that give them the right to just end run those laws and lock people up? Give me a break! [It] seems this War on Drugs often does more harm than the drugs themselves."

Five days later, McWilliams was dead.

McWilliams, the owner of Prelude Press, was the multi-million-copy-selling author of *How to Survive the Loss of a Love, The Personal Computer Book,* and *DO IT! Let's Get Off Our Buts* (with co-author John Roger), a #1 New York Times bestseller. He also wrote what is widely considered to be the definitive book against "consensual" crimes, *Ain't Nobody's Business If You Do.*

He joined the Libertarian Party in 1998 following a nationally televised speech at the Libertarian National Convention in Washington, DC.

> "Not only do we attempt to drag personal morality into the public arena; we put it into the hands of the least efficient organization on earth: government bureaucracy."
>
> —Peter McWilliams,
> Ain't Nobody's Business If You Do

In that speech, McWilliams said, "Marijuana is the finest anti-nausea medication known to science, and our leaders have lied about this consistently. [Arresting people for] medical marijuana is the most hideous example of government interference in the private lives of individuals. It's an outrage within an outrage within an outrage."

McWilliams' death was also noted by Libertarians in his home state.

Sheriff Bill Masters

"Peter McWilliams was a true hero who fought and ultimately gave his life for what he believed in: The right to heal oneself without government interference," said Mark Hinkle, state chair of the California Libertarian Party.

"His loss opens a gaping hole in the fabric of liberty, but his memory will live on not only in the hearts of grateful Libertarians but also in the lives of the countless patients who will take up the crusade for health freedom." —Libertarian Party

We need to remember that every war will claim its victims. Sometimes the victims will be totally innocent, caught in the crossfire. Other times we'll discover, too late, that "enemies" like Peter McWilliams were really the ones fighting on the side of justice. In cases like this, peace is the only sane policy.

The Sheriff chats with a group of youngsters in Grand Junction.

Chapter 2
Getting Our Priorities Straight

A FEW YEARS AGO I was invited to attend a meeting of investigators from all over the nation who were working on a serial murder case. We met at the FBI training academy in Quantico, Virginia. Each of the investigators at the meeting was working on a homicide that we all believed might have been committed by the same person, an ex-police officer. The meeting was arranged by the Child Abduction Serial Killer Unit (CASKU) of the FBI.

This unit has been featured in some recent books and movies where hundreds of agents with large computer banks bring up pictures of suspects and track their movements with satellites until they catch the guy in the act of committing one of the gruesome murders. So it was a bit disappointing when I realized that the unit is in fact just a few overworked FBI agents and clerks whose desks are piled high with folders full of pictures of mutilated young bodies. The happy young faces in the "before" pictures had become missing, tortured, and murdered children.

Sheriff Bill Masters

During the breaks in our meeting I wandered through the building. Hundreds of good-looking, bright, enthusiastic young people swarmed the hallways. They were all going through the FBI academy training.

At lunch we would all go up to the large cafeteria in the academy building, once again surrounded by a sea of new recruits. On one occasion I sat with one of the CASKU agents to drink coffee. I commented that maybe when all these new recruits graduated from the academy, the CASKU unit might get some more help investigating the crimes that drive fear and despair into every parent's heart, if their child is missing for even a moment while at the park or shopping mall.

The agent said, "Sheriff, these aren't FBI agents—they are all DEA agents. The Drug Enforcement Administration is using the FBI Academy to train more agents for the drug war."

I REALIZED I HAD FAILED MY COMMUNITY
BY NOT CAREFULLY ANALYZING THE PROBLEM.
I HAD BECOME PART OF THE DRUG HYSTERIA.

Through the rest of the day the CASKU agents and I went over homicide cases as pictures of murder victims flashed on a screen. The next day on the plane home I stewed silently and thought: What kind of peace officer, what kind of society would allow a peace officer to use one minute of time, spend one dollar, or use any jail cell for a marijuana smoker, when vicious child murderers are on the loose?

After being a drug warrior for many years—and being good at it—after receiving the DEA's award for outstanding achievements in the field of drug law enforcement, I realized I had failed my community by not carefully analyzing the problem. I had become part of the drug hysteria.

Using what Glenn Frey called the "politics of contraband," I had used the drug war to get re-elected. I played the tough guy, but not on the hard ones: the murderers, burglars, thieves, the rapists; no, I had played that hard guy on the easy ones, the dopers. Busting these people is not rocket science. It's a lot easier than—God forbid—getting stuck with a "whodunit" like investigating missing children, burglaries, or murders.

A million Americans are arrested each year for drug violations. Then 40, 50, who really knows how many billions of dollars a year are spent on fighting the drug war, while the CASKU unit looks for thumb tacks to put up one more missing, smiling face on their wall.

I don't know about medical marijuana; it may just be a ruse to get marijuana legalized. But I do know that if I am ever so unfortunate as to catch a disease, I am not going to consult the law books; I am going to consult my doctor and then I will decide—not the Sheriff, not the Chief of Police, not my Congressman, and not the

> "[D]ecades of studies [show] that treatment is far more effective in reducing drug use than are midnight raids, jails, informants, wiretapping, racial profiling, property confiscation, border interdiction, and the shooting down of planes over Peru..."
>
> —Ralph Reiland, Robert Morris College
> Liberty Magazine, July 2001

DEA—but I will make the decision what is best for my body. This is a God-given right that no one should take away. My body, my decision.

If someone is a doper, that is his problem. Get a life, deal with your problem. Some might say to me, "Sheriff, you just don't care about these people anymore." But I do care.

I want people to proudly accept the fact that they alone can change their lives. Our current "bust them and dry them out" policies do little more than enable people to continue their self-destructive life-styles. We need to clearly tell and show people through changes in the law that their dependency is not the drug dealer's fault any more than it is the fault of the bartender, the pharmacist, the tobacco grower, the police officer, the judge, the government, or their mother.

Let's try something new, like telling people to accept responsibility for themselves. Shocking to no one but the current political parties in power, most people will, if given the choice, take care of themselves!

BY ALL MEASURABLE CRITERIA, THE CRIMINAL JUSTICE SYSTEM HAS FAILED TO CONTROL THE DRUG SUPPLY AND WILL CONTINUE TO FAIL IN THE FUTURE.

Those of us who are true peacekeepers should be outraged at the racism of the drug war. Blacks make up 13 percent of the population, 35 percent of the drug arrests and 76 percent of the inmates who are in prison for drug offenses. Few white people go to jail for long periods of time for drug offenses, if they get caught at all.

Let's face it—if you are the President's wife and have a drug problem, you get a drug rehab clinic named after you. If you are poor, Black, or Hispanic, you will languish in jail for years. This is an outrage that tarnishes every lawman's badge in this country.

Our current law enforcement tactics for controlling drugs do little more than create job opportunities for new drug dealers every time we arrest an old one. The supply of illegal drugs seems to never end. In fact, during the past 25 years, illegal drugs have increased in potency and quantity, and the distribution systems have spread from the cities to every town and village in the nation. Our policies have succeeded in making a bunch of punks, who couldn't run a garden hose without instructions, so fantastically wealthy that they now influence politics in America and in foreign nations.

Law enforcement leaders must be truthful with the public and admit that by all measurable criteria, the criminal justice system has failed to control the drug supply and will continue to fail in the future.

A few years back I was speaking to a Los Angeles police officer, proudly telling him how we were conducting road blocks on our rural highway in order to stop the crack cocaine from coming into our county. He just laughed in my face and said, "What are you going to do, Sheriff, build a wall?"

I realize now that our existing situation, as bad as it may be with the crack, meth, heroin, pot, GHB, ecstasy, or whatever, is not as bad as what I see coming over the horizon tomorrow. Unless policies change, the future is one filled with designer drugs like the meth that can be made today, at home, from supplies obtained from the local convenience store. These new drugs may be made anywhere by anybody who attended a high school chemistry class. The supply will be endless and the police will be completely overwhelmed, as if we are not already.

> "In our 'free country' over 750,000 people are now in jail for consensual crimes... [A]nother 2 million are now on parole or probation; over 4 million more will be arrested this year; we will spend $50 billion this year... It's your money. You're paying for it."
>
> —Phil Donahue

Take a walk in my shoes or any lawman's shoes and you will see liberty mostly alive and well, but the corresponding virtue of responsibility is ill and dying.

"We the people" have given up and the government has taken up the responsibility for personal protection, for charity, for health, for children's education, for retirement, for moral guidance, for conservation, for substance addiction, for abusive domestic relationships—to name but a few. Of course government has made a mess of all of them. But what did we expect?

I trust the Nature Conservancy more than I do the Forest Service, I trust my IRA more than I do Social Security, I trust the Salvation Army to give to the truly needy more than I trust the Department of Social Services, and I trust my informed choice over what is right for my children more than I do anyone else's.

LIBERTY, RESPONSIBILITY, AND COMMUNITY.
THAT SHOULD BE THE MOTTO FOUND ON
THE SIDE OF EVERY POLICE CAR IN THE COUNTRY.

We abdicate the responsibility for issues such as drug abuse, spousal abuse, and raising children. We turn these responsibilities over to a deliberately Godless government, but then we are astonished when government programs can't solve these fundamentally moral and spiritual problems.

Our churches and spiritual advisers have abdicated their responsibilities as much as the rest of the public has. When did you last see your minister walking among the crack users, outside of bars at closing time, in the jails in the morning? They sure can preach to the choir. But they tell me, "Sheriff, you've got to stop these drug users." They are calling the wrong guy. We should be calling them.

Today, the criminal justice system no longer supports the concept of enforcing personal responsibility for violent conduct. Instead, it supports the excuse-making industry made up of counselors, drug rehab centers, half way houses, and the like. Cops know that most criminals blame someone or something else for their own actions:

mothers, fathers, wives, girlfriends, the police, drugs and alcohol. Surprisingly, the criminal justice system buys into these excuses and fails to punish people for their criminal behavior.

Let people put whatever they want into their bodies. But demand that any aberrant conduct that hurts or endangers others be judged harshly.

People tell me: Look at the mess we are in, mobs of men attacking women in broad daylight, people caught in the crossfire of drug-dealing gangs, missing and murdered children, insane drivers, and drugs and guns in every government school. Is this what the Libertarians want, they ask?

No, this is not libertarianism. This is our existing society which has been born in the unholy union of failed Republican and Democratic government programs, paid for by the sweat and labor of the American people.

> "The costs to our society have been grievous. Long mandatory minimum sentences have filled our prisons with nonviolent drug offenders and made them, and their families, damaged beings for the rest of their lives. The war on drugs is a testament to the human capacity for self-delusion."
>
> —Anthony Lewis
> New York Times, May 1, 2001

Unlike the others, the Libertarian Party stands for Liberty, Responsibility, and Community. That should be the motto found on the side of every police car in the country.

A recovering drug addict and alcoholic once told me, "If you hang out in a barber shop, you are going to get a haircut." That's what I tell the youth of my county, and they get it. They know better then anyone about drugs, especially the ones like Prozac and Ritalin given to them by their doctors, schools, and mothers.

Estimates are that 20 percent of our children go to school every day high on legal prescription drugs. The medical drugging of our young people is one of the biggest disgraces in the history of this nation.

Some people are just not meant to sit in a classroom for 16 years. A little more than a hundred years ago the young people were the heroes of the day. They were the cowboys and pony express riders, the young mariners on the ocean and the builders in a land abundant with freedom and opportunity. Today we would drug many of those heroes into conformity.

THE MEDICAL DRUGGING OF OUR YOUNG
PEOPLE IS ONE OF THE BIGGEST DISGRACES
IN THE HISTORY OF THIS NATION.

During my last campaign a number of young people came up to me on the street and said, "You're Sheriff Bill Masters! I just wanted to meet you. I wasn't even going to vote till I heard your message. It's nice to hear someone speak the truth."

It appears to me that today's young people have a strong libertarian streak in them. They don't trust government and believe they don't need government to care for them or direct them. They don't want to work five months a year just to pay taxes, and they don't want to be enslaved to pay for the older generation's retirement.

As Libertarians and elected officials, we must listen to the young people in our communities and respect them enough to tell them the truth they seek, for they are the salvation of our nation.

Scott the Addict

Scott was a tall kid with long, unkempt hair. I think of him as a kid even though he was close to 30. He just looked young. His father was American Indian. Scott would have had dark skin, but he was pale and dying. He had been arrested for stealing a pair of gloves from the market. It was cold outside, he said, and his hands hurt. The officer arresting him found a single dose of heroin in his pocket. Normally he would have gotten just a ticket or maybe an overnight stay in jail for the gloves, but the heroin was the kicker.

In Colorado, the possession of any class I drug (heroin, coke, meth, LSD, mushrooms) is a major felony. The crime is the same no matter what amount of drugs you have, or whether you were selling to kids or just had it for yourself. You could have a truckload of meth in front of an elementary school and get charged with the same class of crime that Scott did. The bond was set at $15,000 for a guy who had to steal a $10 pair of gloves.

> "The government's war on drug users is subverting public health, ruining the neighborhoods of millions of Americans, and setting precedents for expanded government power in other areas."
>
> —James Bovard
> Lost Rights, page 199

Scott had been a real pain before he got arrested. He wasn't committing any crimes, but he was really sick. I was a volunteer on the local ambulance service, and we were always getting called to help him. He had some horrible physical problems. Diseases, bleeding out of every orifice, kidneys shutting down.

Sheriff Bill Masters

If you want to learn to stay away from drugs and alcohol, just spend some time on an ambulance service. All Scott wanted when we showed up was some drugs. But we were just a basic service and the hospital was 70 miles away. We would try to make him comfortable for the hour and half trip to the ER. We would drop him off, then wash down the entire rig and ourselves. Scott had no money, so the hospital would kick him out after a day and he would come back to town. Every week or two we would repeat the same trip.

Now Scott was in jail, and he was very sick. He really wanted out. Scott informed on his drug supplier, and the local police got enough to get a search warrant for the guy's house. They found some drugs and busted the guy. The dealer posted bond and took off.

Meanwhile Scott sat in the jail. I had to keep him in isolation, because of the hepatitis and God knows what else he had caught from sharing needles with other drug addicts. I would go in and check on him every day and talk for a few minutes. He told me that his father had been a state trooper in New England. "He drank hard, every day of his life. Still does, even on duty, and no one ever caught on."

Scott informed me that, like his father, he pretty much always used booze but liked using heroin as well. I always have a hard time telling the difference between a down-and-out alcoholic and a heroin addict. They both smell, act, and look the same to me. But the system sends one to treatment and the other to jail.

The jailhouse doc told me that there was nothing anyone could do for Scott and that he was going to die in our jail. The county was spending about $5,000 a month on drugs and doctor bills keeping him going. He knew he wasn't going to make it much longer and kept on asking me to let him go home to New England to die. I found his father, the now-retired state trooper, living alone in an apartment on the East Coast. Dad sounded sad; life had not gone well for him either. He had no money to help Scott, but of course he was welcome to come and stay with him.

I went to the DA, an intense young man, who told me I had to keep Scott in jail because he needed him to testify against the dealer the local police had busted. I argued that Scott wasn't going to be around to testify anyway. My words fell on deaf ears. "The law's the law, Sheriff—you're just getting too soft on these people," the DA told me with finality.

Rockefeller was getting what he wanted, even out here in the West. We were giving the guy a life sentence—a short one, but life in jail it was going to be. I appealed to the judge, who with her legal wisdom told me, "He did a bad drug." Modern justice at its best: no bad people, just bad things.

Money talks. In this case it was the government's money. Take one small county, $5,000 a month in medical bills, and a few well-placed press releases, and things start moving. Scott was let out of jail after doing four months and

> "How can we justify letting violent criminals go because of overcrowding, when there are so many people behind bars whose only crime is that they're addicted to something? Drug addiction is a health problem; it should be treated medically, not criminally."
>
> —**Minnesota Governor Jesse Ventura**
> **Do I Stand Alone? page 157**

promising to return to testify against the dealer. As he signed the promise to return he started to laugh, and his laughter turned into a bad fit of coughing.

"I only wish," he said.

I bought him a $99 train ticket back to New York and gave him a little cash for food. But he never made it home.

He was found dead at Central Station.

Chapter 3
Drug Dealer Whack-A-Mole

EVERY SO OFTEN, we see a picture in the paper with some police officers and a pile of drugs. Great! Another drug bust. Now, this time, we're really "winning the war on drugs." Yeah, right. That's what they've been saying for the last 30 years. The more drug dealers are busted, the more prices are raised, and the more incentive there is for others to deal drugs. Ask the seasoned drug warriors if we're winning the war on drugs. Most of them, during their moments of self-honesty, will admit we're not. As long as there's a demand for drugs, there will be a supply. Meanwhile, we lose more and more of our rights and we lurch toward becoming a police state.

The title for this chapter came to me when I remembered playing that amusement park game Whack-A-Mole. The little mole sticks his head up, and you beat him down. Just when you get that part down, two moles stick their heads up at once, then three. The game keeps going until your quarter runs out. We've spent billions of dollars so far, and the money hasn't run out yet.

Rick the Stick

"When a bust goes down, the price goes up." That was Rick the Stick's "business" motto. The Stick was one of those local guys who always made his living dealing. He was a tall, thin man—hence his name—who liked to ride his bicycle on the highways around Telluride.

I would pass him on the road 70 miles from his home pedaling fast, like he was in a race. I kept thinking that such an athlete must some day see the evil of his ways or understand how harmful drugs were, and stop. He never did.

Over the years Stick had dealt every kind of drug he could get his hands on. He was good at it. He never sold to anyone he didn't know well. He always kept his ear to the ground about who got busted so he could cut them off, lest he get stung by a former customer forced into working for the police.

We ran a number of undercover officers at him, but he never took the bait. He knew all about entrapment, conduit, and other legal issues relevant to street-level drug dealing. Years after I first met him he told me from a jail cell, "I never offer drugs to anyone. I make them come to me and ask, make them ask again. I tell them that I am not a drug dealer, but I have a friend who will sell only to me. I take their cash, leave, and come back with the dope but no cash. If I got busted I would claim I was just doing a guy a favor, then I would turn in some other dealer."

This was his *modus operandi* on first-time sales and we never got to him. Years later he told me one more rule: "I never transport the dope in a car. I always use my bicycle; cops never stop you on a bike."

Stick would also work for me doing dope buys from other dealers when he was short on cash or wanted to stick it to his competition. No matter how much dope he sold, Rick never had any money. As is the case with most street dealers, Rick's own addictions usually got the better of him.

In my zeal to bust dope dealers, I easily overlooked Stick's own dealing. I tried to make myself believe he was serious when he told me he had seen the light. I would pay him some money from the county coffers, which I had to hide in other expenditures lest the Board of Commissioners or the press find out about my little drug-busting operations.

All this worked out really well for Stick. He got some money from the sheriff's office and helped bust his competition. With every arrest, Stick raised his prices. He even increased his inventory prior to the fall of a competitor, knowing that he would have to supply more customers.

Stick would also call me up and tell me, for a fee, where thieves were holding stolen property and who had broken into what business. At times he was quite a crime fighter, and at those times I was happy to have him in my corner.

> "Despite enormous increases in arrests, it was was apparent that arrests neither cured users nor discouraged pushers. New pushers were on the street dealing before the cell doors closed on their predecessors."
>
> —Joseph D. McNamara, NYPD, Retired
> After Prohibition, page 119

Stick's girlfriend was a terrible alcoholic. It was interesting to me that with all the other drugs around, she and Stick would most often be found sucking down Buds, or later, drinking cheap vodka straight. It got so bad that Stick would call us and report his girlfriend was incapacitated by alcohol. We would go over to whatever dump they were living in and find the woman passed out, dead drunk. I had deputies go around to all the liquor stores and bars with a picture of the drunk telling them not to sell to her. Rick started controlling his drinking, but she never could.

One night Stick and his neighbors, who were a bunch of drunks, got into a dispute after they had given his girlfriend some booze. He had come home and found her once again passed out drunk. Rick went over to the neighbors' house and struck one of them in the head with a hammer, which left a nice, round dent about the size of a half-dollar in the guy's skull.

STICK CAME OUT OF THE DARKNESS SCREAMING AND SWINGING AN AXE AT MY HEAD... I ENDED UP GRABBING THE AXE, AND... WE GOT STICK IN HANDCUFFS.

I decided that I had better go have a talk with Stick about hammering on people. So in the pitch dark I walked over to the half-trailer, half-lean-to structure that Stick called home. As I was walking up to the door with a deputy trailing behind me, Stick came out of the darkness screaming and swinging an axe at my head. I was so close I didn't have the time or the quick-mindedness to shoot him. I was between Stick and Jim, the deputy, or Jim might have shot him.

I ended up grabbing the axe, and after a brief struggle we got Stick in handcuffs. He stated later that he had thought I was the guy he had clobbered with the hammer, and he had made up his mind to finish the job. He said, "I am just pissed that he keeps on giving her booze."

One time we were able to get a wiretap order on a group of cocaine dealers' telephones. A state narcotics task force was conducting the case but wanted to make it seem like they were cooperating with the locals, so they let us know what was going on.

The wiretap was a real pain. First, the affidavit to get the order was about 500 pages long. Most people think the government can tap anyone's phone, but in reality it's difficult to get legal permission to listen to people's phone calls.

But the biggest irritation is then having to listen to, record, and document all the calls. We had to rent a condo, install ten reel-to-reel recorders, run ten lines into the condo, and staff the "wire condo" with two officers around the clock for months on end.

The undercover officers staffing the phones were brought in from Denver, and they lived in the condo. During their off hours they would hang out around the hot tub of the condo complex. Women living in the complex, or tourists, would show up at times and get in the tub with them, but there were strict rules about not screwing around. So the undercover cops had to distance themselves anytime women showed up. It was soon rumored around town that the guys living in the wire condo were all gay, which really pissed off the officers.

> "I have served as a magistrate judge for more than 19 years. During that period I have issued hundreds of drug-offense search and arrest warrants... I have asked the affiant DEA agents the question: 'Are we winning the war on drugs?' To this date, I have never received an affirmative response."
>
> —Judge William F. Sanderson, Jr.
> Why Our Drug Laws Have Failed, page 48

One of the court-imposed rules about listening to a phone call was that if after three minutes the conversation had not turned to the subject of importing or dealing cocaine, the officer listening to the call had to hang up his connection and listen no further. The reel-to-reel tapes were set to help automatically enforce this rule, as they would shut off as soon as the headset was turned off.

The dealers were aware of these legal requirements. So, being cautious, they spent several minutes talking about the weather, skiing, trips they'd taken, or sex before turning to the subject of dope dealing. One guy would go on and on about whom he had dragged home the night before. In lurid detail he would describe what he and the woman or women had done to each other during the night's encounter. We figured it was all just bravado until some incoming phone calls were received from the women inquiring if our suspected dealer had as good a time as they had. Telluride's a fairly small town, so the information about who was involved in these escapades, as well as the lurid details, was a lot more than I needed to know.

UNFORTUNATELY FOR HIM, HE ALSO INQUIRED...
HOW MUCH IT WOULD COST TO TRANSPORT
THE "ACRES" TO LOS ANGELES.

One cocaine importer got a little too clever. He started talking about drugs in code words as soon as the phone was answered. He wanted to know about Colombian "real estate." How much it was "per acre." Was the "land" high in quality. Unfortunately for him, he also inquired, during the first three minutes of the conversation, how much it would cost to transport the "acres" to Los Angeles.

After months of listening to these kinds of calls, a bust was planned and raiding officers searched a number of houses. A small amount of cocaine was seized at one house (about a gram, or one-twenty-eighth of an ounce), and eight ounces were taken from another house. The state narcotics strike force brought in television news crews to film the arrests.

Drug War Addiction   Drug Dealer Whack-A-Mole

The "kingpin" of the drug ring, in whose home we found the gram of coke, was given eight years in jail by a judge who, in front of a crowded courtroom, stated he wanted to send a tough message to drug dealers. Half a year later, in a quiet "reconsideration hearing" in another county, the same judge reduced the sentence to six months and let the "kingpin" out of jail.

The state narcotics task force members stated that a major source of cocaine had been eliminated and that the good people of Western Colorado could rest easy knowing that the cocaine supply had been stopped. Further, they promised more arrests: they had uncovered just the "tip of an iceberg." The cost of the operation was estimated at half a million dollars.

Rick the Stick just kept his ear to the ground and raised his prices.

"The next time you hear the drug czar proclaim success, just say to yourself: 'They can't even keep drugs out of prisons.'"

—Sheldon Richman
Future of Freedom Foundation
Rocky Mountain News, June 29, 2001
http://www.fff.org/editorial/ed0701f.htm

Chapter 4
Police Integrity: A Post-Mortem

OUR POLICE DEPARTMENTS suffer corruption as a direct result of drug prohibition. The most obvious problem is that police officers can make big money dealing drugs, protecting drug dealers, or simply looking the other way.

But drug prohibition also creates problems that aren't so obvious. Because drug abuse harms the user, usually there's nobody around to complain to the police about people using drugs. For crimes like rape and theft, the victim is usually more than happy to assist the police in finding the criminal. That's not often the case with drug abuse. Even the most strident prohibitionists think the people they know who use drugs, such as their friends and children, are exceptions to the general rule and should be treated with compassion rather than served with a hefty prison sentence. To bust drug dealers and users, police have to be more—shall we say—proactive.

Sheriff Bill Masters

How do police make a bust in drug cases? Often we send out undercover agents to buy drugs. It's a horrible thing to buy or sell drugs—unless you're a police officer. Then we play semantic games to pretend our actions aren't entrapment. Pity the poor fool who never thought about selling drugs until approached by an undercover officer offering fistfuls of cash.

In order to make it easier for police to punish drug dealers, politicians passed laws allowing asset forfeiture for drug cases. Today, across America, police don't even have to charge you with a crime in order to take your property. They can take your cash, boat, car, house, or whatever, and keep it!

BANKING CLERKS AND POSTAL EMPLOYEES ARE REQUIRED TO REPORT YOUR UNUSUAL FINANCIAL ACTIVITIES TO THE FEDERAL DRUG POLICE.

How do the police get away with that? After all, the Fourth Amendment to the U.S. Constitution states, "The right of the people to be secure in their persons, houses, papers and effects, against unreasonable searches and seizures, shall not be violated..." Here's the trick: the police charge your property with committing the crime, and then they take the property. No kidding. Property doesn't have Constitutional rights. Perhaps coincidentally, expensive cars and fancy houses seem to "commit" more crimes than junker cars and dumpy houses.

If you carry around "too much" cash, police just assume you're a drug dealer. Banking clerks and postal employees are required to report your unusual financial activities to the federal drug police. In his book *Lost Rights* (page 11), James Bovard tells the story of Willie Jones. Willie took $9,000 with him from Nashville to Houston to buy some plants for his landscaping business. After he bought his plane ticket with cash, the ticket agent reported him to Drug Enforcement Agency officers. Those officers searched Jones and took his money but didn't arrest him. Willie said, "I didn't know it was against the law for a 42-year-old Black man to have money in his pocket."

That raises another issue. While people of all ethnic and racial backgrounds have been robbed, abused, or killed over the drug war, people of color are especially harmed. Because police have to go looking for drug offenses, profiling is an inevitable tool of the drug warrior. Racial profiling is all too common. The term "driving while Black" is uncomfortably familiar. When officers become numb to the routine humiliation of some, they risk falling into increasingly brutal behavior toward all citizens.

> "Today, every bank customer is a suspect. If a financial institution has reason to believe a transaction is out of the ordinary for that person, it must submit a 'suspicious activity report'."
>
> —Robyn Blummer,
> St. Petersburg Times, July 24, 2001

Unfortunately, some prohibitionists who are loath to narc out their white neighbors or kids are less reluctant to turn a suspicious eye to Blacks or Hispanics. While only a small minority of police officers are racists, the drug war gives that group a pretext to put their bigotry into practice.

Because of the flagrant violations of privacy rights pushed by drug prohibition, many good people won't even consider police service. Those who take an honest look at the racial injustice of prohibition, the insane rate of prison expansion for non-violent offenders, the billions of dollars of expenses, and the loss of civil rights, are less interested in serving as a peace officer. While the majority of our officers are quality people who genuinely care about protecting the innocent, the number of "bad apples" has increased in direct proportion to the escalation of the drug war.

Decades ago, most people viewed the police as their friends and protectors. Now a strong minority, if not a majority, of people view the police with suspicion. In too many cases, people look at cops with anger or hatred.

The rift drug prohibition has created between the police and the public is one of the saddest results of our policies. Peace officers across the nation feel in their hearts that something is amiss, and I believe more and more of them are realizing just how insidious prohibition really is.

The Lure of Easy Money

I was approached by a man who claimed he knew of a drug deal going down. Unlike most informants, he didn't want anything from me. Neither he nor his girlfriend was in trouble with the law, and he didn't want any money. He just didn't like drugs. He was a stand-up citizen who believed he was doing the right thing. So he told me what he heard.

A load of meth was coming in from California. He knew the whole story: who was picking up the load, the type of car being used, the date it was supposed to come in, where it was going. Good stuff. With a little bit of computer work I found out about the people doing the deal. They lived over in a neighboring county, where the meth was going.

I have known the sheriff in the other county for years. He's a "good ol' boy," 6'2", 280 pounds, huge hands, cowboy hat, always eating corn on the cob with a big grin at the county fair. A conservative Republican sheriff in a conservative Republican county. We were friends in a way, not socially, but we would help each other out in a pinch and never say a word about it. Rural sheriffs are just that way.

I called up the sheriff to give him the information on the meth deal. The sheriff was out, so I talked to a deputy. I told the deputy the story about the drug deal going down, and when I got to the names of the people involved the phone line went silent. I felt like I was talking to myself. I asked, "You guys going take care of this?"

"Yeah. Don't worry; I'll call the sheriff and we'll get on it," the deputy responded. I told the deputy that I was going to set up a road check to look for the load car, that I figured it was coming in through my county sometime in the next 24 hours.

After I hung up, something bothered me about the call. I wrote up a report and sent a copy of it off to the local Colorado Bureau of Investigation (CBI) office. I know the CBI can't do any more than anyone else in stemming the flow of meth, but I wanted someone else to know about the case.

> "[B]lack market profits will be used to corrupt law enforcement—not only prison guards, but policemen, customs officials, judges and the military."
>
> —Sheldon Richman
> Future of Freedom Foundation
> Rocky Mountain News June 29, 2001
> http://www.fff.org/editorial/ed0701f.htm

I never heard another word about the meth load. My deputies never spotted the load car. Neither the sheriff nor the CBI ever called me back.

A whole year went by before I finally got a message to call a CBI agent. Jack, the agent, used to be the sheriff in still another county, then he went to work for the state.

Most state and federal law enforcement agencies are great at doing undercover drug cases in small counties, making a big splash, then packing up and leaving just as the case turns bad. Maybe they raided the wrong house, or their undercover operative turned out to be a bigger crook than the guys they busted. Lawsuits start flying, the press starts knocking at the door, and the local sheriff gets stuck with the mess while the feds are off drinking beer in Denver, looking for the next small-county law enforcement sucker they can "help."

Fortunately, Jack is different. Having been a sheriff himself who worked with all of us, he knew not to burn bridges.

THE LOCAL SHERIFF GETS STUCK WITH THE MESS WHILE THE FEDS ARE OFF DRINKING BEER IN DENVER...

Jack asked me if I was ever looking for a car that was bringing meth in from California. I told him about my information from the previous year. I said I'd told the neighboring sheriff's office that they had a load coming into their county, and I mentioned the report I'd sent to the CBI office.

Jack asked me for more details and requested another copy of the report. (The previous report was "filed" somewhere.) After so many years in the business he knew not to ask where my information had come from. I knew I shouldn't ask why he needed the information now, twelve months after the load came in.

Jack just said, "I'll tell ya about it someday," which is cop-talk for "keep reading the newspapers." With all the leaks, rip offs, and payoffs, it's best not to know too much about some other agency's drug case, so if it goes bad because someone gets paid off or just has a big mouth, the hounds won't come barking up your tree.

Another three or four months went by before the bust went down. The sheriff, the undersheriff, a couple of deputies, and even the sheriff's kid all got busted for running a meth-dealing ring, or stealing evidence, or both. Just another good ol' boy, dope-dealing sheriff's office.

It turned out that when I gave the deputy the names of the people bringing the meth in, he recognized them as relatives of the undersheriff (a political appointee of the sheriff). He called the sheriff, who called the undersheriff, who called his relatives, who warned the driver of the load car that I was on to them. The driver buried the dope out in the desert and came on home using a northern road, thereby avoiding the road checks I set up in my county.

Later, when they figured the heat was off, they went out to the desert and dug up the dope. They sold it around the Western Slope of Colorado. They would have gotten away with it, too, except somebody got caught holding some of the meth. In order to get a lighter sentence, that person told the CBI agents about the cops' involvement. If you need to rat off somebody, why not doper cops?

That bust was a sad day for Colorado sheriffs. Nobody wanted

> "Law enforcement agencies are major beneficiaries of the drug war at the same time that law enforcement is a major victim. The agencies benefit from the many billions of dollars spent on pursuing the drug war and from the proceeds of forfeiture, an increasingly attractive and lucrative source of funds."
>
> —Milton Friedman
> **After Prohibition, page ix**

to see a respected member of his own fraternity get nailed in such a way. Some were angry that the affair had tarnished all Colorado sheriffs' badges. Still others simply refused to believe it was true.

But most of us, the ones who had been drug warriors for years, knew that Glenn Frey had the answer in *Smuggler's Blues*: "It's the lure of easy money, it's got a very strong appeal."

Bill Masters, 1971

Chapter 5
The Military
and Foreign Intervention

From the halls of Montezuma, to the shores of Tripoli,
We will fight our country's battles, in the air, on land and sea

I grew up in a Marine household. My father proudly served in the South Pacific during World War II. When I was young, I remember looking through old pictures of warships in action and young Marines in the jungle standing next to my father. I am proud of him. I am proud of the Marines. I served in the Coast Guard, and I am proud of them. *Semper Paratus*, always ready.

In boot camp we were taught the traditions of the Coast Guard: the landing craft at Normandy, the life-saving rescues, braving the most dangerous seas and the darkest nights. "You have to go out, but you don't have to come back." That was the motto of the rescue boats.

I read through my old Coast Guardsman's manual the other day and there is not a word in it about marijuana, cocaine, heroin, or illegal immigrants. I looked at the Coast Guard web page and today it proudly lists the amounts of drugs seized this year: 69,194 pounds of cocaine, 20,338 pounds of marijuana. Also listed, as if they were just another commodity, were "1,990 alien migrants" seized.

The web page also told a story about seizing a fishing vessel from Belize with over 20,000 pounds of cocaine on board. The seizure took place in the Eastern Pacific, 1,500 miles south of San Diego. I am sure some wonder whose coast they are guarding.

First to fight for right and freedom and to keep our honor clean

Which brings me back to the Marines and their proud tradition of fighting our country's battles. The Marines are going to have to add another line to their hymn after running into Zeke Hernandez. Zeke, you'll remember, was an 18-year-old high school student who stumbled upon a group of camouflaged and armed U.S. Marines assigned to Joint Task Force Six drug interdiction team. The Marines shot and killed young Zeke, mistaking him for a drug runner.

Our flag's unfurled to every breeze from dawn to setting sun
We have fought in every clime and place, where we could take a gun
In the snow of far off northern lands and in sunny tropic scenes
You will find us always on the job, The United States Marines

I haven't found the place where the Marines are going to insert the line, "And Joint Task Force Six Drug Interdiction Team!"

Joint Task Force Six is based at Fort Biggs Army Base at El Paso, Texas. The job of the task force is to work under the policy guidance of the Office of National Drug Control Policy, coordinating federal, state and local law enforcement agencies and military force support to counter drug operations. Using Marines and other soldiers, the force may deploy small squads of men along the U.S. border with Mexico. The group reportedly has deployed several hundred men at a time. Their primary mission is to observe and report activity. However, as with the case of Zeke, at times things go wrong when armed solders confront civilian populations.

A number of people believe the Constitution prohibits the use of the military to enforce civilian laws: it does not. Although most Americans want to think that the military is used for defending our country, to "fight our country's battles," in fact the Army, Navy, Marines and even the Coast Guard are on a direct collision course with the citizens of this country.

> "The militarization of law enforcement has created the equivalent of a standing army engaged against the American people— precisely what was feared by the Framers."
>
> —David B. Kopel
> After Prohibition, page 88

Historically, the military has been used a number of times to put down minor civilian uprisings. In 1787 the Army was used to put down Shay's Rebellion in Massachusetts; in 1794 it was the Whiskey Rebellion. In 1807 Congress declared the Army to be the enforcer of all federal law. In 1846 the Army restored order during the anti-Catholic riots in Philadelphia and did the same again in the 1850s "Bloody Kansas" battles between free and slave staters.

In 1854 Attorney General Caleb Cushing ordered the Army and Navy to enforce the Fugitive Slave Act to return escaped slaves to their owners, presumably because many local officials in the North were against slavery or found it politically undesirable to assist slave owners in recapturing their "property."

In 1859, then-Colonel Robert E. Lee commanded Marines to capture John Brown at the Harper's Ferry Arsenal during his failed attempt to arm slaves. Lee turned Brown over to Virginia authorities, who then tried and hanged him.

In 1863 anti-draft riots in New York City were put down by troops fresh from the battle of Gettysburg, and, of course, federal troops occupied and policed the defeated South for twelve years, from 1865 till 1877.

It was the close election of 1876 that caused the passage of the Posse Comitatus Act, which limited the use of the Army on U.S. soil. Rutherford Hayes, a Republican, won the presidency in 1876 by only one electoral vote after winning in three hotly disputed Southern states, one of which was Florida. President Grant had sent federal troops into the states to oversee the election. A Democratic Congress, upset at losing the election and facing the intimidation of having federal troops stationed in certain key states, voted in the Posse Comitatus Act of 1878:

Whoever except in cases and under circumstances express by the Constitution or Act of Congress willfully uses any part of the Army [or Air Force (added later)] as a posse comitatus or otherwise to execute the laws shall be fined under this title or imprisoned not more than two years, or both.

Black's Law Dictionary defines posse comitatus as "The posse of the county. The power or force of the county. The entire population of a county above the age of 15 which a sheriff may summon to his assistance in certain cases, as to aid him in keeping the peace or in pursuing and arresting felons."

Congress prohibited the Army from acting as a posse that might be used to enforce laws on the civilian population, unless of course Congress gave it the okay.

It is interesting to note that the Congress left the Navy and the Marines out of the posse comitatus law. The Coast Guard, which is a part of the Department of Transportation, has always been authorized to enforce various federal laws and is allowed to routinely arrest civilians.

Still later, the Department of Defense policy and regulations, 10 United States Code 375, subjected the Navy and Marine Corps to the same posse comitatus restrictions imposed on the Army and Air Force.

However, to get around the law, when the Navy wants to stop and search a civilian vessel for drugs, it raises the Coast Guard Ensign (flag), thereby morphing the naval warship into a Coast Guard cutter for the express purpose of meeting the requirements of the Posse Comitatus Act and 10 USC 375. Coast Guard officers take "tactical control" of the Navy warship during these operations.

> "Congress should...
> [r]epeal the drug
> exceptions and other
> exceptions to the Posse
> Comitatus Act. Retain
> exceptions only for law
> enforcement in international
> waters or requiring unique
> military expertise related
> to nuclear weapons."
>
> —**David B. Kopel**
> **After Prohibition, pages 86-87**

It is doubtful that the Congress is aware of these quick-change games being played out on the high seas by our honorable Naval commanders. Frankly, being a Coast Guard veteran, I didn't believe it until the practice was readily confirmed by the Coast Guard law enforcement office. Then again, these types of ruses are commonplace in civilian police/military resource relationships.

Sheriff Bill Masters

With the down-sizing of the military, large amounts of equipment became available to civilian police agencies if they would agree to use it to fight drugs. Everything from file cabinets to M16s could be obtained. My own department obtained several pairs of snowshoes, which we gave to our search and rescue group. It wasn't hard to convince the powers that be that snowshoes must be part of any law enforcement agency's coordinated attack on drug dealers.

THIS LEADS ME TO BELIEVE OUR STATE MOTTO OUGHT TO BE THE SAME AS THAT OF THE LADIES ON EAST COLFAX: "WE DO ANYTHING FOR MONEY."

The list of military hardware given to local police forces between 1995 and 1997 includes 3,800 M16 fully automatic assault rifles, 73 M79 grenade launchers, and 112 armored personnel carriers. In 1997, a total of 1.2 million pieces of military equipment was given away, and this equipment ended up in the hands of our local police to be used to fight the war on drugs.

Police agencies often claim they need military equipment because of the increased amount of firepower the crooks have that makes police work so much more dangerous. But according to the FBI uniform crime reports, the number of police officers killed in the line of duty is the lowest it has been in 35 years. In 1999, 42 officers out of an estimated 600,000 armed police officials in this country were murdered. The chance of being murdered on the job is probably greater for convenience store clerks in some areas than for police officers.

National Guard forces are exempt from the Posse Comitatus Act because they are considered to be state-armed forces under the command of the governor of each state. An aide to Colorado

Governor Bill Owens told me recently that the Department of Defense pays for 90 percent of the cost of running the Colorado National Guard. And to quote the aide, "If we don't agree to use them (the Colorado National Guard) to fight drugs, we won't get the money to run our helicopters or anything else." This leads me to believe our state motto ought to be the same as that of the ladies on east Colfax: "We do anything for money."

According to *National Defense,* the journal of the National Defense Industrial Association, the U.S. National Guard forces have 126 rotary and fixed-winged aircraft dedicated to fighting the drug war. They are deployed in 32 states across the country for counter-drug operations. The Guard is also looking into new technologies, including unmanned aerial vehicles, for use in the domestic war on drugs.

Another disturbing trend is the increased use of civilian contractors to perform law enforcement and military-style operations against drug dealers in foreign countries and here at home. Companies like DynCorp, according to *National Defense,* "provide the State and Justice departments with a one-stop-shop counter-drug support expertise." The company supports drug-war operations at both the front and back ends, employing everything from airborne crop-dusting in Colombia to asset forfeiture experts who work at 385 Justice Department sites in the United States. The company currently has a $316 million contract for management of

> "The image that outraged me... was the cover of a news magazine from the mid-1980s. Workers in a cocaine field were piled like firewood, their white peasant clothing red with blood. They had been gunned down in cold blood by American troops... The headline blared: Winning the War on Drugs."
>
> —Peter McWilliams
> *Ain't Nobody's Business If You Do*

the Justice Department's "asset forfeiture program." This private company has been involved in more than 60,000 asset seizures in the United States. They conduct "criminal-intelligence collection and analysis, forensic support and asset identification and tracking."

Private drug war contractors were involved in the recent murder of Roni Bowers and her baby, Charity. The contractors, flying a plane owned by the U.S. military, conspired with the Peruvian Air Force to shoot down the plane that Roni, Charity and other missionaries were flying in.

DRUG CONTROL AGENCIES ARE HELPING THE PERUVIAN GOVERNMENT SHOOT DOWN PLANES... THEY CAN'T DO IT HERE, OR THEY WOULD BE CHARGED WITH MURDER.

There is a reason why the United States drug control agencies are helping the Peruvian government shoot down planes in that country. It is because they can't do it here, or they would be charged with murder.

In this country we don't allow people to be shot just because they are suspected of something. That would be uncivilized, against our rule of law.

So what does our government do? Just like when the Navy flies the Coast Guard Ensign, government finds some way around it. Congress, the President, and our drug control agencies are acting like the Sopranos. "Can't cap him here, too many people around. Let's go to Jersey." You begin to wonder who the real thugs are.

Rolling Stone published one of the most disturbing articles I have read in a long time. It is a story of gangster cops in the LAPD. Not just a handful but groups of them were murderers, drug couriers, gang members, and bank robbers. And the leaders tried to cover it all up. Most of the crooked cops were assigned to special anti-drug and gang units. Those cops betrayed the public trust, and some remain on the job.

The honest LAPD lawmen and women are demoralized. Their numbers are down by almost 1,000 officers. They can't recruit enough new cadets to fill academy classes, even when they continue to lower their standards and accept employees with criminal backgrounds. A recent Police Protective League poll shows that two-thirds of the officers want to quit their jobs.

In May of 2001, the *Charlotte Observer* reported that the Federal Drug Enforcement Administration agents in the San Juan Office were instructed to file false reports in order to obtain more funding from the DEA. It's estimated that 70 percent of the arrests listed by the office were phony. One DEA agent reported that he was instructed to read the local newspaper looking for names of people who were arrested by the local police. The

> "In the last 15 years, the United States has spent $30 billion, most of it in Latin America, trying to cut the supply of drugs from abroad. The costs to other societies have been severe: the rise of drug gangs, the suffering of peasants from crop eradication, the corruption of governments."
>
> —Anthony Lewis
> New York Times, May 1, 2001

agent would then make out DEA arrest cards with the name from the newspaper, showing an arrest by his office.

After being instructed to arrest only people who possessed more than 11 pounds of cocaine or 50 pounds of marijuana, agents continued to arrest people for a few grams of cocaine or an ounce or two of marijuana in order to show that drugs were out of control and that more agents were needed in their office. During the period of false reporting, arrests doubled each year from 652 to 1,136 to 2,042.

The office also reported that, with the help of U.S. Marines, it destroyed Bolivian crops consisting of 672,577 mature marijuana plants and 4,540,203 seedlings. Whistle-blowing DEA agents stated that it was impossible to count plants with such precision.

Using the fraudulent figures, the San Juan DEA administrator convinced Congress to give more money to the San Juan DEA office so it could address "a public safety crisis in Puerto Rico." The San Juan office doubled its staff to 304 agents, and the administrator was promoted to head the 500 agents in the international division of the DEA.

Those agents who complained to superiors about the fraud were transferred.

It's like the Quakers say: in any war you become like your enemy. Vicious, liars, corrupted by money, cowards: these are the attributes that many citizens associate with both drug dealers and the police.

Our military forces and their proud heritage will be the next victims of our misguided polices if they get caught in the quicksand of the drug war.

Here's health to you and to our Corps which we are proud to serve.
In many a strife we've fought for life and never lost our nerve.
If the Army and the Navy ever look on heaven's scenes
they will find the streets are guarded by the United States Marines.

A Mexican "Drug Lord"

Some years ago I took a couple of weeks off and traveled around Mexico, practicing my limited Spanish. I was never one who could sit around a beach for long, so I spent the weeks traveling around by bus and train, visiting small villages and enjoying rural Mexico.

At one point I boarded a train leaving from Los Mochis on the Mexican west coast. The train was going over the mountains of northern Mexico to the desert city of Chihuahua. I had heard the trip through the mountains was spectacular. I looked forward to escaping the dusty, hot city of Los Mochis.

I arrived early in the morning at the train station and got a seat on the train. Then I walked up and down the platform looking at all the people saying good-bye to relatives. I spotted one group of women waiting on the platform near the entrance of the station. They wore colorful Indian dresses, a bit like the ones I had seen on the Navajo and Hopi women of Northern Arizona but with lighter colors, almost white, and adorned with embroidered flowers. The women ranged in age from ancient to middle-aged to teenagers and even children. One beautiful girl, barely a woman, held a small baby in her arms. They all kept looking at the door leading from the station to the platform, straining their necks to see over the crowd.

> "56 die in Colombian drug fight—Fierce jungle fighting in Colombia's main coca growing region killed 30 soldiers and 26 leftist guerrillas on Friday, the army said—the heaviest casualties since a U.S.-backed anti-narcotics offensive got under way late last year."
>
> —Rocky Mountain News, June 23, 2001

Suddenly one of the younger ones let out a cry and they all looked toward the door as two thin teenage boys dressed in brilliant white cotton shirts, black pants and straw cowboy hats came through the door. Both were handcuffed.

Two men escorted them. One was an overweight, middle-aged man who wore, even in the sweltering heat, a heavy blue police-type coat with gold buttons and a fake fur collar. The other escort was a younger man who wore a muscle-man T-shirt that had "UCLA" written on it, jeans that looked three sizes too small, and several gold chains around his neck. These were the uniforms of the feared "federales." Each wore a cocked-and-locked, .45 caliber semiautomatic pistol haphazardly stuck in his waistband.

Graciously, the officials stepped back and allowed the two boys to be swarmed by the women, who bestowed them with little gifts of food and two small, homemade backpacks which had twine for straps. In the packs were some bananas, candies, small pictures of Jesus and the Virgin Mary, maybe a pair of socks and some other items I could not see. Strapped to the top of each pack was a small pillow embroidered with names, shapes of animals, stars and moons.

ONE OF THE YOUNG MEN IN HANDCUFFS HELD THE BABY FOR A MOMENT, TENDERLY... WHILE THE TEENAGE MOTHER KISSED HIM DELICATELY ON THE CHEEK.

One of the young men in handcuffs held the baby for a moment, tenderly, but with effort due to the handcuffs, while the teenage mother kissed him delicately on the cheek. After a couple of minutes the officers moved back in and escorted their prisoners onto the train. As we pulled away from the station, the young mother stood on the platform and waved the baby's hand at us until we were out of sight.

I returned to my seat to find it occupied by the sweating fat guy in the police coat. Next to him was the guy in the UCLA shirt, and across from them in the seat facing the rear of the train were the two compensarios in handcuffs.

I moved my bag, sat across the aisle from the quartet, and tried some of my Spanish on the officers. I told them I was a cop, and we were soon like long-lost brothers. We chatted in broken English and

Spanish for most of the trip. The two prisoners never spoke a word.

The fat guy was in charge, and he could speak English fairly well. He told me he was part of a special anti-drug squad that had been trained and funded by the U.S. government. Proudly, he informed me that they had even been to Washington, D.C.

The younger officer told me that their job was to fly around in Hueys supplied by the United States and drop in on dirt-poor farmers who were growing opium poppies in the mountains. "We are all armed with machine guns but we never shoot people in the back," he said.

With this comforting information in mind, I asked him about their two prisoners. He replied that the two boys had been caught growing poppies on their small farms. He explained that the land was poor and not much besides some corn would grow. However, drug manufacturers would pay farmers well for growing poppies for the American heroin market.

Both of the federales said they couldn't care less if some farmer was

> "Were police to see themselves primarily as social peace-officers, they would be less inclined to 'overkill' in their dealings with both ordinary citizens and those whose disruptive activities properly require their intervention."
>
> —John Kleinig, Ethicist
> After Prohibition, page 88 (quoted)

making a few bucks from gringo drug addicts. However, the United States was paying them to bust these guys, so... A shrug of the shoulders revealed the rest of their feelings. The two boys had been sentenced to eight years, and the officers were given extra pay to transport them to the pen at Juarez.

After a while the conversation drifted off, and after it got dark I fell asleep. Once I opened my eyes and saw one of the boys pulling a piece of bundled wax paper out of his backpack. The paper was tied with a green and white bow. Inside were some light brown homemade cookies, shaped in the form of hearts. He silently offered them to his handlers, who each took one without a word.

After we got to Chihuahua, the officers hustled the two prisoners over to a white Ford pickup truck with a camper shell and a bad muffler. The young men were told to get into the back under the camper shell, and the federales crowded into the front with two other officers who had been waiting for them. The truck roared away down the dusty street leading north out of Chihuahua.

The next day, on the way to the border, the bus I was on went by the Juarez prison. As we passed, no one looked at the tan-colored, 30-foot high walls.

The white pickup was parked outside the main gate.

Chapter 6
Drug Warriors
Tilting at Windmills

"...I have done, am doing, and shall do the most famous deeds of chivalry that the world has ever seen, can see or will see." —Don Quixote

They caught sight of some thirty or forty windmills, which stand on that plain, and as soon as Don Quixote saw them he said to his squire: "Fortune is guiding our affairs better than we would have wished. Look over there, friend Sancho Panza, where more than thirty monstrous giants appear. I intend to do battle with them and take all their lives. With their spoils we will begin to get rich, for this is a fair war, and it is a great service to God to wipe such a wicked brood from the face of the earth."

"What giants?" asked Sancho Panza.

—Cervantes' *Don Quixote*, translated by J.M. Cohen

Sheriff Bill Masters

Don Quixote was a decent guy, just very confused. Reminds me of some drug warriors I know. Unfortunately, a lot of times prohibitionists get so caught up in acting morally superior, they lose sight of reality. In this chapter, I address a number of faulty arguments made in support of drug prohibition.

Does repealing drug prohibition mean the government sanctions drug use?

We've all heard it: when legislators don't want to worry about whether a law will actually work, they vote for the law to "send a message," often "to our children." If drugs were decriminalized, the drug warriors tell us, that would mean the government condones drug use.

That argument just doesn't stand up to serious thought. Killing yourself with cigarettes is legal. Clogging your arteries with high-fat food is legal. Destroying your liver with alcohol is legal. Wasting your life in front of the television is legal. As a lawman, I support none of these activities. Yet they should remain legal.

Never forget that when legislators pass a law, they are automatically giving authority to men with guns to enforce the law. Thus, we should pass only those laws which are really necessary.

Morality isn't the same thing as the law. The law touches on only limited aspects of morality: protecting people and their property from physical harm and preventing theft and fraud. Morality is much broader than the law. When we try to make the law as big as morality, laws become profuse, ambiguous, unknowable, flaunted, and unenforceable. Ultimately, morality loses much of its meaning when government agents start enforcing it at the point of a gun. And the really important laws get lost in the shuffle. Drug prohibition isn't "getting tough on crime;" it's preventing police officers from getting tough on real crimes.

In fact, it's immoral of politicians to press their personal morality upon the broad citizenry. A free country such as America demands tolerance. Once politicians, along with their armies of bureaucrats and armed enforcers, start to act as the morality police, there's really no way to draw a line in the sand.

A moral system of laws prevents people from hurting each other but leaves them free to otherwise pursue their own lives. Being moral means taking responsibility for our own lives and for our communities. Pretending politicians will solve our moral problems for us is a false hope and is itself an abnegation of personal responsibility.

If you want to know the "message" politicians are sending to our children with the drug war, here it is: it's okay for armed enforcers to kill innocent children like Zeke Hernandez and Charity Bowers, if they believe drugs may be present. It's okay for police to bust down your door in the middle of the night with submachine guns

> "Protecting our children from drugs is the most compelling reason to legalize them. The only way to keep drugs out of our schools is to take the profit out... The War on Drugs doesn't protect our children, it encourages pushers to sell to them."
>
> —Dr. Mary Ruwart
> http://www.self-gov.org/ruwart/

locked and loaded, if some drugged-up, paid informant said there might be drugs around. It's okay for police to take your property without even charging you with a crime. It's okay for politicians to wipe their feet on the Bill of Rights, as long as they're doing it in the name of getting tough on drug dealers.

That's the "morality" of the war on drugs. I wish politicians really would look at the "message" they're sending, instead of getting high on their own power by creating hysteria among the people. Drug warriors act self-righteous, but they're not righteous.

Should government prohibit drugs so people don't drive high?

We don't make alcohol illegal in order to stop drunk driving. We don't make Big Macs illegal in order to stop people from driving with their faces buried in a bag of fast food. Instead, the proper role for police is to bust people who are driving dangerously, whether because of alcohol, other drugs, or sheer carelessness.

If we want to enforce laws about dangerous driving, why do we waste police resources fighting the drug war? Would you rather have a police officer spend his time arresting some pot smoker playing video games in his basement, or patrolling the streets for drunk drivers? Think about it.

With the repeal of drug prohibition, wouldn't everybody turn into crazed drug fiends?

One social truth will always be with us: the large majority of people will handle their lives more or less responsibly, rather than turn to irresponsible drug use. Also, a minority of people will become addicted to alcohol, other drugs, food, television, sex, or whatever.

By chance I flipped on Ollie North's radio show some time ago. He had a guest on who sang the praises of drug prohibition. (The guest made his living enforcing drug laws.) In the most indignant voice he could muster, Ollie said, "If drugs are legalized, we'd have as many drug addicts as alcoholics." (I'm paraphrasing here.) Frankly, I'm surprised at you, Ollie: that's the sort of misleading factoid you'd blast in some other context.

Republicans are funny that way. They claim to support individual responsibility. They claim that, left to their own devices, most people will lead successful lives. But when it comes to drugs, Republicans imagine that, without the help of Big Brother, people will become raving lunatics and America will become a land of mindless zombies.

But deep down Ollie knows people can be responsible for their own actions, even if drugs are available. In discussing his own children, Ollie admitted drugs are already widely available, despite the government's best efforts to eradicate them. Ollie was proud to say his kids don't take drugs. But are Ollie's kids so uniquely gifted that they alone have the power to resist the evils of narcotics, a will the rest of us lack? Is Ollie alone able to teach moral values to his children? I'm sure Ollie is a great father, but he should give the rest of us a little credit, too. In America today, anybody who wants drugs badly enough can find them. Most of us choose not to.

It's interesting how the Republicans and Democrats use the

> "If the Drug War was halted tomorrow morning, the drug use in this country would not change a bit. The only thing that would change is that people would stop getting their heads blown off in the street trying to get their smack on the corner."
>
> —Dave Matthews, Musician
> Rolling Stone, August 16, 2001

exact same arguments, but for different issues. For Republicans, drugs are evil, even "demonic," and they can force people to destroy their lives and go crazy. The Democrats use the same argument, only in reference to another sort of inanimate object: firearms. In both cases, the politicians and zealots ignore the reality of human free will.

Yet, even after we discard the more hysterical arguments, we must address the serious economic and psychological issues surrounding drug use. The basic theory of supply and demand tells us that when prices go down, consumption goes up. Once drug prohibition is repealed and the violent black market is wiped out, the prices of most drugs will drop dramatically. Thus, some addicts and casual users may take more drugs, and some people who don't take drugs today because they're so expensive may start taking them.

But that simple economic model doesn't tell the whole story. Repealing drug prohibition will also result in some people taking fewer drugs or no drugs.

• **Forbidden Fruit.** For some rebellious young people, taking drugs is a way to say "to hell with The Man." As a song by Rage Against the Machine puts it, "F__ you, I won't do what you tell me!" Some people simply do not resist forbidden fruit. The tendency is so ingrained in human nature that it is central to the story of Adam and Eve.

When drug use is de-glorified, taken off the criminal market, and subjected to boring quality controls—when drugs are no longer forbidden fruit—drug use will lose much of its appeal as a way to rebel. For example, drug use among youth in the Netherlands is relatively low, where all drugs are practically legal. The law of supply and demand assumes the item in question remains the same, but repealing prohibition would eliminate the status of drugs as forbidden fruit.

• **Education.** Today, drug education is often a joke. The drug war requires a vast body of deceitful propaganda to sustain it. Basically, we lie to our children about drugs. It's no surprise, then, that many young people ignore even the legitimate warnings about drug abuse. New Mexico Governor Gary Johnson wrote about this issue in the book *After Prohibition*:

We need to have an honest educational campaign about drugs. The Partnership for a Drug Free America was bragging to me that it was responsible for the "Here's your brain, and here's your brain on drugs" ad. Well, some kids believe that, perhaps three-year-olds, maybe some nine- or ten-year-olds.... Like everybody else, I was also told that if you smoked marijuana, you're going to go crazy. You're going to do crime. You're going to lose your mind. Then you smoked marijuana for the first time and none of those things happened.... And then you realize that they weren't telling you the truth. That's why I envision advertising that tells the truth, which says drugs are kind of nice and that's the lure of drugs. But the reality is that if you continue to do drugs, they are a real handicap. (18)

The use of crackpot propaganda is nothing new to prohibition. James T. Bennett and Thomas J. DiLorenzo tell us in their book *Official Lies: How Washington Misleads Us* (pages 219-220) that school children used to be "taught" similar lies in the era of alcohol prohibition. For example, children were taught most beer drinkers die from dropsy, and alcohol turns the blood to water and makes the heart dependent on more alcohol for continued function. And just look at how well alcohol prohibition worked.

> "Just as bootleggers were forced out of business in 1933 when Prohibition was repealed, making the sale of liquor legal (thus eliminating racketeering), the legalization of drugs would put drug dealers out of business..."
>
> —Abigail Van Buren ("Dear Abby")

But alcohol really is dangerous if it's abused, and other drugs can ruin your life. Young people need to understand the very real dangers of all drugs, they need to understand leading a quality life precludes drug abuse. As California Judge James P. Gray sums up in *Why Our Drug Laws Have Failed and What We Can Do About It*, "Drug education for our children, even our young children, must be thoughtful, verifiable, reasonable, and practical—or it will fail" (169).

• **Treatment.** Today, drug addicts are treated as criminals, as social pariahs. Thus, many addicts don't seek the treatment they need. With the repeal of drug prohibition, addicts would be more open about their problem and more willing to pursue treatment options. In addition, if we'd stop wasting billions of dollars on the drug war every year and spend some of that money on treatment, we'd make a lot bigger impact in terms of helping drug addicts.

• **Minors and children.** Many parents fear drug pushers will give drugs to their children. But we don't have this fear about alcohol. Why is that? Alcohol is sold by reputable business owners, while other drugs are sold by criminal street dealers. Addicts who turn to dealing drugs to pay for their exorbitantly expensive habits have few compunctions about selling drugs to kids. In fact, young people often report it's harder to get alcohol than other drugs. With the repeal of drug prohibition, police officers could spend more energy enforcing laws that set age restrictions for the purchase of all drugs, including alcohol.

• **Personal responsibility.** When drug prohibition is repealed, more people will stop pretending the government will solve our country's drug problems. Religious and other spiritual leaders will take responsibility to help people deal with drug abuse. Parents will take more time to talk honestly with their children about drugs. Today, politicians lie to the people when they argue more money, more guns, and more prisons will solve problems of drug addiction. In the future, politicians will tell the truth: "We tried to solve this problem and failed. Now it's up to individuals, families, churches, and communities to take responsibility."

The upshot is that we don't really know what will happen with drug use in this country once prohibition is repealed. The reduced price will encourage more drug use, but other factors will encourage less drug use. It's possible we may see some increase in drug use immediately following the repeal of prohibition, but I expect long-term use to decline below current levels. In any case, the apocalyptic predictions of some drug warriors are completely off base.

> "Murder rates were high during the period of alcohol prohibition, fell after repeal, rose again with increased efforts to prohibit illegal drugs, and remain high."
>
> —David Friedman, Economist
> Liberty Magazine, June 2001

Would the repeal of drug prohibition exacerbate problems of the violent drug market?

Some conservatives make a simple argument that sounds plausible at first: "Look at all the problems with violence we have today. Gangs are murdering each other over drug turf, we have drive-by shootings and stray bullets, and pushers shoot first, ask questions later. If we legalize drugs, these problems will only get worse."

Not only is that argument wrong, it is the exact opposite of the truth. Violence in drug sales is caused by prohibition, not by the drugs themselves. Similarly, during alcohol prohibition, violent gangsters ran illegal alcohol. If we made the drugs coffee or tobacco illegal, prices for both those products would skyrocket and a violent network of criminals would arise to distribute them. Drug prohibition causes street violence in at least four ways.

• **Turf wars.** For no legal business do we see violent gangsters walking around murdering their competition. In the drug trade, that happens all the time. Drug dealers sometimes attempt to forcibly take control of the drug market in a specific area. When that happens, the result is violence.

• **Protection.** As David Friedman writes in his book *Hidden Order: The Economics of Everyday Life*, "Drug sellers have lots of portable wealth in the form of money and drugs, and do not have the option of calling the police if someone steals it. The result is violence by drug dealers defending their property and by other people trying to steal it" (305).

• **Violence training.** People who think they might want to live a violent lifestyle are attracted to the drug trade. Drug dealers then train themselves and others in the methods and instruments of violence. Sometimes this violence carries over into non-drug-related activities.

• **Violence involving police.** When politicians compel the police to make midnight, no-knock, military-style assault raids, drug dealers aren't the only ones to suffer. Sometimes law enforcement officers get killed or injured, too. Sometimes fights between police and drug dealers spill over and take the lives of innocent people. Sometimes the police raid the wrong house and traumatize or kill the innocent people living inside. All this violence is a direct result of drug prohibition.

In his article "Violence and the U.S. Prohibitions of Drugs and Alcohol," published in the Fall, 1999, *American Law and Economics Review* (78-114), economics professor Jeffrey A. Miron of Boston University "examines the relation between prohibitions and violence using the historical behavior of the homicide rate in the United States."

The results document that increases in enforcement of drug and alcohol prohibition have been associated with increases in the homicide rate, and auxiliary evidence suggests this positive correlation reflects a causal effect of prohibition enforcement on homicide. Controlling for other potential determinants of the homicide rate—the age composition of the population, the incarceration rate, economic conditions, gun availability, and the death penalty—does not alter the conclusion that drug and alcohol prohibition have substantially raised the homicide rate in the United States over much of the past 100 years.

> "America woke up in 1933 and ended the 'Noble Experiment'—the nightmare of alcohol Prohibition—that had triggered the worst crime wave in the nation's history. It is long past time to end the even larger crime wave sponsored by drug Prohibition."
>
> **—Harry Browne**
> **2000 Libertarian Presidential Candidate**

Professor Miron estimates the homicide rate is currently 25-75 percent higher than it would be if prohibition were repealed. His charts comparing the homicide rate with the level of prohibition enforcement are telling. Those charts are reproduced below in Figures 1 and 2. The double line in Figure 2 represents slightly different ways of accounting for prohibition expenditures, and it counts only federal funds. In Figure 1, the homicide rate peaks at the height of alcohol prohibition and the modern drug war, respectively.

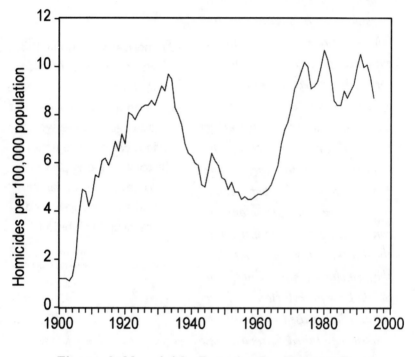

Figure 1: Homicide Rate in the United States

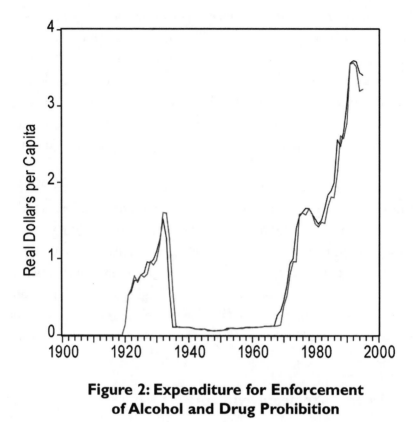

**Figure 2: Expenditure for Enforcement
of Alcohol and Drug Prohibition**

Two articles from the Associated Press serve to illustrate the problem with prohibition. A story dated April 22, 2001, reads, "Philadelphia—An apparently stray bullet killed a youth minister [Nafes Johnson] as he sat in a church van with members of his congregation.... The bullet appeared to have been fired from about a block away in a shooting over a drug deal..." A story just six days later states, "Waterbury, Conn.—A drug dealer was sentenced to 20 years in prison Friday in the slaying of an 8-year-old murder witness and the boy's mother... Leroy 'B.J.' Brown Jr. and... Karen Clarke." I hope the thugs who killed Nafes, B.J., and Karen got what they deserved. But the fact remains that these innocent people would never have been killed but for drug prohibition. The politicians who created the violent black market in drugs share responsibility for those deaths.

Earlier we wondered if repealing drug prohibition would lead to more or less drug use. I think it will lead to less, but even if I'm wrong, I think getting rid of all the violence is worth it. People who abuse drugs hurt mainly themselves. The violence of drug prohibition puts all of us at risk.

The big issue that prohibitionists miss, but as a peace officer I confront every day, is that every dollar and minute spent fighting the drug war is a dollar and minute that cannot be spent fighting violent crime. Drug prohibition consumes billions of dollars every year and millions of hours of enforcement time. If we repealed prohibition and invested even a portion of the savings into fighting real crimes, we'd all be a lot safer than we are today. The poorer neighborhoods in our big cities, which suffer the worst crime, could be cleaned up and made safe again.

Do drugs make people violent?

Do some people get violent when they drink alcohol? Obviously. Alcohol abuse plays a big part in many cases of domestic violence. However, most people drink responsibly and do not get violent when they consume alcohol. Should we return to alcohol prohibition to deal with the small minority of people who become violent drunks? Or should we spend our enforcement efforts dealing specifically with those who commit violence?

Different drugs have very different physiological impacts. If anything, marijuana makes people less prone to violence. Heroin and other drugs in the opiate family like morphine cause people to relax. Cocaine, on the other hand, is a stimulant. (Coffee and tobacco are mild stimulants.) Methamphetamine also causes people to feel more wound up. It is true that some drugs lead some people to act more violently.

However, drugs don't cause problems by themselves: they sometimes exacerbate problems that already exist. If we took all the cases of domestic violence in which the physical abuser also abuses alcohol, and we removed the alcohol, would that automatically fix the problem of domestic violence? Of course not. For some people, drinking alcohol is a step they take before they act out violence they've already planned or anticipated. The same is true for other drugs. On the other hand, an emotionally stable and peaceful person is unlikely to become violent whether or not he or she takes drugs.

Again, police enforcement should target the violence directly. If somebody acts violently, whether or not they're on drugs, the police should intervene. Those people who never get violent when they take alcohol or other drugs aren't a risk. Those who are prone to violence must learn to take responsibility to make sure they either avoid drugs or take safety precautions.

> "Every dollar spent on... drug dealers is a dollar that cannot be spent on... other criminals. Getting 'tough' on drugs inevitably translates into getting 'soft' on all other offenses."
>
> —Judge James P. Gray
> **Why Our Drug Laws Have Failed And What We Can Do About It**, page 69

If anything, drug prohibition results in drugs that are more prone to make people violent. First, because potency and purity of drugs are totally unregulated on the black market, users don't know what they're getting. It may be the equivalent of a person drinking two beers as opposed to chugging a flask of vodka. Somebody may take a drug that's a lot more powerful than expected. Second, as Friedman points out in his article "The Economics of Drug Violence" in the June, 2001, *Liberty Magazine*, alcohol may make violence more likely than, say, heroin. "Prohibition of the latter sort of drug may result in a substitution of the former sort and thus an increase in violent crime" (20).

Lots of drugs are dangerous if they're abused, including ones that are now legal. The problem of people taking drugs and acting violently is a very real one. We'll make more headway against the problem if we spend our resources addressing the problems of violence, rather than wasting effort cracking down on people who aren't violent.

Do Drugs Make People Steal?

Drugs don't turn people into muggers, burglars, and thieves. Instead, some people who are criminals are also drug abusers. Drug addicts do roughly the same amount of drugs (a lot) regardless of cost. When prohibition is repealed and drug prices decline, addicts may buy slightly more drugs but will spend a lot less money on those drugs. Thus, addicts who steal to pay for their drug habit won't steal as much.

Of course, if we offered more treatment and spent more of our law enforcement resources targeting theft rather than fighting the drug war, theft by drug addicts would go down even more. Theft in general would go down if we used police resources more wisely.

Will the repeal of drug prohibition make drugs more dangerous?

Actually, drug prohibition is the main reason drugs are so dangerous today. During alcohol prohibition, some people went blind or suffered other severe health problems because of potent, impure drinks.

During prohibition, drugs are sold by criminals, by the type of people who don't mind using violence on a daily basis. These dealers don't care about the health of their customers. They don't have to worry about getting sued. Thus, illegal drugs are often highly potent and sometimes poisonous. People who buy drugs don't know what they're buying, or what the potency is. Many health problems associated with illegal drug use are actually caused by impurities in the drugs, not the drugs themselves.

Another reality of drug prohibition is that it's easier for criminals to transport highly potent drugs in smaller quantities. Thus, virtually every drug has increased in potency over the years, including marijuana and cocaine. Some drugs were invented as a response to drug prohibition. Drugs like crack cocaine and methamphetamine would probably never have been developed in the absence of prohibition.

> "An estimated 90% of deaths due to overdose of more toxic recreational drugs are caused by tainted formulations and other black market consequences. In the U.S., shared needles are the major cause of the spread of AIDS. The War on Drugs has made a minor health problem into a major one."
>
> —Dr. Mary Ruwart
> http://www.self-gov.org/ruwart/

After prohibition is repealed, the potency of drugs will probably decline and impurities will be mostly eliminated.

It's time to get real about drugs. It's time to seriously address the problems of drug addiction, and it's time to seriously address the problems of drug war addiction. Until we do so, we'll continue to see more violent crime, more dangerous drugs, more corruption in our police departments, and more loss of civil rights. A lot of the problems blamed on drugs are actually caused by drug prohibition. And those problems tied directly to drug abuse are impossible to solve until we get our priorities straight, until we stop tilting at windmills.

Chapter 7
Drug Wars and Gun Wars

THE ANTI-GUN LOBBY raises funds by pointing out the high rate of firearms-related violence in the United States. Unfortunately, both these activists and the politicians ignore a very obvious point: the United States suffers high rates of homicide precisely because of drug prohibition and the violent black market it creates. And Professor Miron suggests that, for the same reason drug prohibitions cause violence, gun prohibitions might do the same thing.

Conservatives who care about the right to bear arms should also care about repealing drug prohibition. Besides the fact that prohibition drives the violence that's behind the sentiment to ban guns, drug prohibition and gun prohibition are rooted in the exact same social philosophy. Instead of regulating violent behavior, prohibitionists want to regulate inanimate objects. Historically, gun control is intimately linked to drug prohibition, as when alcohol prohibition led to the gangster violence, which became a pretext for passage of the 1934 National Firearms Act, the first federal gun legislation to apply to the general population.

Liberals who are sensitive to the injustices of drug prohibition should also be wary of gun restrictions. The same gestapo-like tactics used to enforce drug prohibition will also be used to enforce gun prohibition. The racial injustices and violations of civil rights caused by drug prohibition are exacerbated by gun bans.

Following the murders at Columbine High School, I wrote an essay about civil arms, completed on April 28, 1999. Because of the close links between drug prohibition and gun prohibition, I include that essay here.

Gun Laws After Columbine

I can understand the call for gun control after the atrocity at Columbine High School. However, careful analysis of the problem and history of gun control, violent crime, and the recent shooting is required to make proper decisions to help prevent such criminal acts in the future.

Firearm ownership is a guaranteed right under the Second Amendment to the United States Constitution and is assured to a higher degree in Section 13 of the Colorado Constitution, where it states that no person's right to keep and bear arms to defend his "home, person and property" will be even "called into question."

Ignoring the Second Amendment almost immediately after it was adopted, the federal Congress passed gun control laws forbidding the sale of firearms to Native Americans. These laws were often passed when the government reacted to a hysterical public demanding action after reading gruesome newspaper accounts of atrocities allegedly committed by rogue bands of Indians.

Native tribes were forced to trade with smugglers and criminals who demanded outrageous prices for old and barely functioning firearms. Tribe members took to raiding white settlements in efforts to obtain firearms to protect themselves from a government and a white citizenry bent on genocide.

With Native Americans unarmed and defenseless, the U.S. government felt little threat in ignoring treaties with tribes when the white public demanded more land. Eventually an entire race of people was largely wiped out. Try to wrestle a rifle out of a Navajo's hands today and he will probably shove the stock down your throat and then give you a bag to carry your teeth around in.

After the Civil War the white people in the South (and in many cases the North) passed several different gun control laws designed to keep firearms out of the hands of the recently freed African-Americans. Klan-type raids on African-American communities were frequent, and the "brave" white knights of the order just could not stomach the thought of anyone resisting a lynching. Today, African-Americans can call the local police for help when threatened.

> "In some states, free and/or enslaved blacks were disarmed by law in order to maintain their servile condition. State legislation that prohibited blacks from bearing arms... ignored the fact that the United States Constitution... referred to the bearing of arms as a right of 'the people'..."
>
> —Stephen P. Halbrook
> That Every Man Be Armed, page 97

Germany was a civilized, developed country 60 years ago. Art, culture, and the rule of law were important to the German people. In a peaceful, civilized country, why would any citizen need a firearm? Only the police needed handguns and, except for a few hunting rifles locked up in sporting clubs (Gentiles only, please), no one was armed. No one needs a firearm, the friendly guy in the brown shirt said. We are just trying to protect you.

Then six million defenseless children, women and men were marched to their deaths. Couldn't happen here. Not in a civilized country like ours. But I know more than one Jewish guy who says "Never Again" more like a battle cry than a remembrance of the departed.

GOVERNMENT LAWS AND PROGRAMS SELDOM WORK THE WAY WE WANT THEM TO... I DON'T THINK THIS COUNTRY COULD STAND ANOTHER PROHIBITION PROGRAM.

Generally, government laws and programs seldom work the way we want them to. One only has to look at the $30 billion a year war on drugs to determine how effective a war on firearms will be. The drug war has brought us arrests on the order of a million people a year, gang-related mass killings, and drugs that are available in every town, city, and school. The drug war makes standing in line at the post office look like the model of government efficiency. I don't think this country could stand another prohibition program.

Government polices at times work against the reasonable efforts to control firearms. In the mid-1970s, the federal government was trying to implement different gun control measures as a result of a series of mass murders by lone gunmen. Charles Whitmen had killed 18, chiefly using a hunting rifle, and wounded 30 in Austin, Texas. Jimmy Essex killed 10 and wounded 17 in New Orleans. At the same time, a man named Carlos Garcia received a loan from the federal government's Small Business Administration to start a retail firearm business. Garcia quickly expanded into manufacturing the TEC-9 pistol, widely regarded as a poor quality gun, which is the precursor of a gun used in the Columbine shooting. TEC-9s are also on the Bureau of Alcohol, Tobacco, and Firearms' Top 10 list of most-often investigated firearm.

England has had the strongest gun control laws in the West for years, yet the firearm-related atrocities there have been horrific. On March 13, 1996, Thomas Hamilton walked into his local school in the village of Dunblane, Scotland. Surprisingly, given Great Britain's gun control laws, he had four handguns on him. Hamilton walked down the hallways until he found the smallest children, 5- and 6-year-olds, playing nursery games in the gym. He then shot and killed 16 of the children and their teacher, before killing himself. This was the worst shooting in Great Britain since 1987, when a 27-year-old man shot and killed 16 people and himself in Hungerford, England.

News reports lead us to believe that the current string of murders is a modern phenomenon. Few records exist, but these include some reports of historical mass murders. Heldne Jegardo in Brittany, France, poisoned 23 people in the early 1800s. Van der Linden in Holland poisoned over 50 people in 1852. In 1862 Martin du Mollard of Paris stabbed 10 people to death. On September 6, 1949, Howard Unruh in New Jersey shot and killed 13 people with a 9mm handgun, and in 1958 Charles Starkweather killed 11 people with a pistol in two days.

Of course large numbers of people can be murdered by using some means other than firearms. The Oklahoma City bombers used

> "The controversial ban on the ownership of handguns which was introduced after the Dunblane massacre has failed to halt an increasing number of crimes involving firearms [in Great Britain]."
>
> —David Bamber, Telegraph, July 16, 2001

common fertilizer to build the bomb that killed 168. Prior to that terrible day, the largest mass murder in U.S. history was carried out in New York by Julio Gonzalez who, using less than a dollar's worth of gasoline, set fire to the Happy Land Social Club in 1992, killing 87 people.

What all this leads me to believe is that tyrannical governments want an unarmed population, that gun control doesn't work, that many government programs work against one another, and that mass murderers are at least clever enough to use poison, make explosives from common materials, set fires, or use whatever other means are available to commit their evil deeds.

Politicians, responding to the public's frustrated cry, will want to institute government programs that, cruelly, will only give us a false sense of security. New feel-good laws will be passed that will further restrict people's rights, cost more taxpayer money, and expand the role of government. None of the proposed regulations would have prevented the Littleton disaster, and none of them will have any real effect on the prevention of future atrocities.

I WANT ALL PEOPLE TO... PROUDLY ACCEPT
PERSONAL RESPONSIBILITY FOR THE WELL-BEING
OF THEMSELVES AND THEIR FAMILIES.

As an option, we in the law enforcement community can rationally, through the study of the criminology and victimology of these incidents, determine what, if anything, can be done to minimize the risk to the children, and then of course release that information to the public so they can make informed decisions about the safety of their children.

Being the father and stepfather to four great kids, as well as being a Libertarian and the elected sheriff of San Miguel county, I can tell you that this event affected me deeply. I want the world to be safer for the kids, and therefore I want our society to address the root causes of crime. I don't want empty promises or politically self-serving speeches from the President about "Why don't (children) use words instead of weapons," while our bombs are falling on villages in a faraway land. I don't want more laws added to the 33,000 robotic-type laws that currently attempt in vain to control human conduct in Colorado.

I do want the ability to choose where my children are going to be and which school they should attend. I want parents to have the time to be responsible for their kids rather than having to work five months a year just to pay taxes.

I want a society that doesn't let kids grow up in the hopelessness and despair of a welfare state and then enter an economy where the government has crushed opportunity. I want all people to be held accountable for their actions and to proudly accept personal responsibility for the well-being of themselves and their families. Until we address some of these root causes of crime, our society will continue to breed criminals, and no permanent solution to crime will be found.

> "One who values his life and takes seriously his responsibilities to his family and his community... will be armed... and will defend himself when faced with lethal violence."
>
> —Jeff Snyder,
> Nation of Cowards:
> Essays on the Ethics of Gun Control

The Sheriff is greeted by the Pro Second Amendment
Committee at its annual banquet, March, 2001.

Chapter 8
A Spiritual Matter

EARLY IN 2001, my wife Jill went to England as part of a cultural exchange for her work. I tagged along. After we returned home, some people we met there read some of my comments about the "spiritual problem" of drug abuse, and they asked me what I meant by that.

Drug abuse is just one symptom of a widespread problem. When people abuse drugs, they are acting from the assumption that happiness is something that just happens to you. Joy in a pill.

Drug abuse can be especially destructive for addicts, but it is only one of many ways a person can lead an empty life. Some people expect sex to make them happy, so they roam from conquest to conquest without ever finding contentment. Others waste vast amounts of their time vegetating in front of the television. For some, food is an obsession.

Sometimes, American education teaches kids passivity, that life is something to be endured and, when possible, escaped. Kids don't need drugs in order to turn off their minds.

The Oxford English dictionary defines "spirit" as "the animating or vital principle in man... that which gives life... the breath of life."

What animates you? Why do you get up every morning? People who don't have a ready answer to those sorts of questions, or don't at least try to come up with answers, start to go dead inside. If you're spiritually dead, it doesn't make much difference what you do with your body.

PROHIBITIONISTS PRETEND THAT CONTROLLING
A PERSON'S ENVIRONMENT WILL SOMEHOW SOLVE
THE PERSON'S SPIRITUAL DILEMMAS.

Philosopher Tara Smith prefers to speak in terms of people flourishing rather than just "being" happy. "I... use 'flourishing' because 'happiness' has a more passive connotation. That is, people often think of happiness as something that does or does not happen to a person, with the person entirely on the receiving end of this fortuitous event. 'Flourishing,' in contrast, suggests action. It reflects not just a feeling of satisfaction with one's experience, as happiness does, but also a person's own activity as the chief source of that feeling" (*Viable Values*, 125).

If you're waiting for happiness to just walk up and smack you, you'll be waiting a long time. True happiness comes from taking charge of your life, setting worthy goals, and working toward those goals. The Founders wrote of "life, liberty, and the pursuit of happiness" for a reason: it's a journey, not a destination. And happiness must be earned.

Most people live a mixed lifestyle, sometimes taking an active role in flourishing, sometimes expecting the world to hand them happiness on a silver platter. Drug addiction is the ultimate consequence of the notion that happiness is divorced from action and from a person's character. When a person feels so empty inside, all those drugs are supposed to fill the void. Ultimately, abusing drugs is like drinking sand when you're dying of thirst.

The policy of drug prohibition only reinforces the notion that people are driven primarily by external things. Just look at the ridiculous hysteria surrounding drugs. Some people act on the presumption that drugs have some sort of supernatural power to corrupt people. In fact, a person of strong character, of strong spirit, wouldn't feel the slightest temptation to abuse drugs regardless of circumstances. It's not as if we don't all face a multitude of other temptations every day.

> "The avoidance of consciousness is clearly evident in problems of addiction. When we become addicted to alcohol or drugs or destructive relationships, the implicit intention is invariably to ameliorate anxiety and pain—to escape awareness of one's core feelings of powerlessness..."
>
> **—Nathaniel Branden**
> **The Six Pillars of Self-Esteem, page 81**

The prohibitionists believe they can make people happy from the outside. What's more, they avoid taking true responsibility to extend a helping hand to others and instead rely on the force of government to command compliance. Prohibitionists pretend that controlling a person's environment will somehow solve the person's spiritual dilemmas. When prohibition fails, when people still abuse drugs because they haven't resolved their internal conflicts, the prohibitionists get mad and call for even greater use of force. Instead of examining their own beliefs, prohibitionists rush to adopt an external "solution."

What drug addicts and prohibitionists have in common is a tendency to blame the outside world for their problems and lack of contentment, and when the external device fails, they angrily turn to it again and again while knowing ahead of time it will never really work.

"This time, shooting drugs into my vein will make me happy."

"This time, chasing down drug users with guns drawn will make society a better place to live."

Nathaniel Branden comes close to what I mean by spirituality:

> If spirituality *means pertaining to consciousness and the needs and development of consciousness, then whoever commits to awareness and personal growth as a way of life—which entails, among other things, self-awareness and self-examination—is on a spiritual path.... Whoever continually strives to achieve a clearer and clearer vision of reality and his or her place in it—whoever is pulled forward by a* passion *for such clarity—is, to that extent, leading a spiritual life. (The Art of Living Consciously, 181)*

The Lost Keys

The darkened room was filled with computer screens displaying radio tower signals and the status of various emergency equipment. LED lights flickered on and off around the room. It was late. The crew was burning through the seventh hour of a twelve-hour shift. Calls slow down that time of day until about 6:00 a.m., when people start moving around again.

The 911 phone rings in a different tone. When it's quiet the staff plays a game to see who is the fastest at answering. This time, Mary wins.

"What is your emergency?" A young woman was on the other end of the phone. A man at her house had stopped breathing. Drug overdose. Before Mary even answered the phone, the computer screen had displayed the address where the call originated, and it showed which police, fire, and ambulance service had responsibility for that location. Mary moved the computer mouse automatically and clicked the pointer on the Placerville Fire-Ambulance icon.

The computer system commands the radio to send a two-tone code out of an antenna from the sheriff's office. Another computer and antenna on top of a 12,000-foot peak acts as a relay station, which broadcasts the tones into more than a dozen darkened homes around the area. There, the volunteer firefighter and ambulance crews are jolted out of their beds. You can't make these pagers play soft music or set them to vibrator mode. If the screaming tones don't get the volunteers scratching at the ceiling, Mary's booming voice surely will.

> "Addiction is more likely to occur among people who believe the drug is stronger than they are, that is, who believe they are addicted... Addiction occurs when people come to rely on a drug or an experience as a way of coping with problems... when it provides a false sense of power, control, and self-esteem..."
>
> —Carole Wade and Carol Tavris
> Psychology, page 601

My wife Jill is a paramedic. She and I bolted out of bed with the first blaring tone and the call about the "man not breathing." We quickly dressed in wool sheriff's sweaters and ran out to my patrol car. On the radio we got a few more details. Mary was still on the line with the caller trying to instruct her on how to do mouth-to-mouth rescue breathing.

It sounded bad. We decide to go straight to the scene. We passed a number of our volunteer firefighter neighbors going the opposite way, small red lights flashing on their vehicles, headed off to the fire station to get the ambulance.

According to Mary's computer screen the house sat on a dirt road off the highway, a quarter mile behind some other homes. She guided us on the radio. When I pulled into the driveway, a number of young people were waving their arms. I told one of them to go to the highway and direct the ambulance in.

We were led into a back bedroom, where a young man, 18 or 20 years old, was lying on the bed, white as the sheets, not breathing. I have seen it before, and it doesn't look good.

I REACHED MARY ON MY HANDHELD AND ASKED HER TO CALL THE CORONER. SUDDENLY THE GUY SPRANG UP OUT OF BED, RESURRECTED AND PISSED OFF.

Jill went to work on him with the help of Joyce, another medic who came straight to the house. Jill stuck an IV line in his arm while Joyce put an airway down this throat and started bagging him.

The room filled up with firefighters in yellow bunker gear dragging a gurney in with them. Jill drew some Narcan from a small bottle into a syringe and then injected it into the IV line. "Stand back! He's going to come out of this quick and maybe fighting," she told us all. I whispered, "Yeah, right." I reached Mary on my handheld and asked her to call the coroner.

Suddenly the guy sprang up out of bed, resurrected and pissed off. He was dragging IV tubes and O2 lines and acting like he wanted to fight. All of us jumped on him, including a few firefighters wearing helmets and bunker gear. Jill started taking him down as he began to understand what happened to him. We put him on the gurney and rolled him out to the ambulance.

I started looking around for the heroin. Most of the young people had disappeared. The woman who'd called in, a 20-year-old living in the house with her mother, said the patient and another guy had just driven in from Texas about an hour earlier. She said she knew the guy from high school but had no idea he was now "into" heroin. The guy's partner, Paul, claimed he didn't know he was using heroin, either.

Paul told me, "He just went into the bedroom and never came out, so I went in and checked on him and found him passed out."

"Dead, you mean."

"Yeah, I guess."

"You guess?! Not breathing means dead to me."

"Yeah, I guess."

"What did you do with his kit, his syringe and cook spoon?"

"What?"

"What, what! It's a simple question."

"I don't know"

"You don't know what you did with it?"

"No... No... I just don't know."

Okay, I figured, at least they didn't wait any longer to call or dump the guy off on the doorstep of the clinic—or worse, my house.

> "The moral virtue is a mean... between two vices, the one involving excess, the other deficiency..."
>
> "[H]appiness is activity in accordance with virtue..."
>
> —Aristotle
> Nicomachean Ethics

I drove Paul up to the clinic, about a half hour away. We talked about drugs and why people do them. He still didn't know, but he said, "I know it sounds stupid, but movies like *Pulp Fiction* make it seem like it's okay, almost cool to do it."

I looked at his face in the passing lights. He just stared straight ahead, but I believe him. Movies, dope, and violence—it all reminds me of a quote from Socrates. "You write the laws and I'll sing the songs, let's see which the people remember."

The OD kid was released after being in the clinic for a few hours. We all shrugged with the unspoken words, "Hope he learned something." Exhausted, we headed for home.

IT ALL REMINDS ME OF A QUOTE FROM SOCRATES.
"YOU WRITE THE LAWS AND I'LL SING THE SONGS,
LET'S SEE WHICH THE PEOPLE REMEMBER."

Like he always does, our old dog had fallen asleep in the entryway blocking the door. After some pushing and coaxing she got up, gave me a dirty look, and sleepily plopped down again a couple feet away. The sunlight was beginning to peek over the horizon, but we slipped back into bed anyway. After a few minutes the girls came in, getting ready for school and fighting over the bathroom. We have two bathrooms, but for some reason they have to use ours. A few minutes later the boys, Lane and Bailey, climbed into our bed, Bailey on his mom's side and Lane on mine.

The phone rang. It was Mary. "Sheriff, the kid who OD'd last night called and said he can't find his keys."

I didn't know whether to laugh or cry.

Chapter 9
Simple Laws: Pathway to Freedom

A SUPREME COURT JUSTICE once defined the Second Amendment as "the palladium of liberty."

That word he used, palladium, refers to the statue Pallas Athena, whose preservation was believed to ensure the safety of the ancient Greek city of Troy. To the people of Troy, the statue was a shield, a safeguard against their enemies, and as long as she stood guard no harm could come to them.

My question to conservatives is this: Have you taken up your duty, not just to guard the Second Amendment, but are you truly the shield, the protector, of the beautiful but fragile lady we call liberty?

Do you stand beside those who are harassed and arrested because of the color of their skin? Do you sit back while your neighbors are dragged off in the middle of the night for what they choose to put into their bodies? Do you honorably and respectfully uphold the rights of others to speak their truth no matter how opposed it is to yours? And do you oppose excessive taxes even if their proceeds would line your pockets?

Liberty is a harsh mistress. You cannot pick and choose what you like and dislike about her. Liberty will not change her principles for you, no matter how much you claim to love her. She will stand fast in her demands for total acceptance. If you can't receive her, she will recognize you as a false lover and leave you. And when you hear that door slam, it will take every tear in your eye, every ounce of blood in your veins, and all the nerve in your heart to win her back.

LIBERTY IS A HARSH MISTRESS... LIBERTY WILL NOT CHANGE HER PRINCIPLES FOR YOU, NO MATTER HOW MUCH YOU CLAIM TO LOVE HER.

Now, being a Libertarian, I have a problem with the drug war. Personally, I just don't care what people put into their bodies. I care about their actions. If they hurt or endanger someone, if they violate someone's property, they should be held accountable to the law. And the law's reaction should be swift, severe and certain.

Instead of enforcing the laws that protect lives and property, last year we arrested 700,000 people for possession of marijuana. In the history of mankind it has never been documented that marijuana has ever caused the accidental, negligent or deliberate death of anyone. A government that can put over half a million of its citizens in jail every year for possessing a little relatively harmless plant can do anything it wants.

And I don't care who the president is, Republican or Democrat, the peaceful, law-abiding, American gun owner is next.

If you like the effectiveness of the war on drugs, 700,000 people arrested, 30 billion dollars a year, more police cars, more courts, more jail cells and drugs on every street, government school and even in the prisons, you are going to just love the war on firearms.

A few years back we were remodeling the old jail in Telluride. When the jail was constructed in the late 1800s, the builders first made the iron cell block, which included solid metal walls with barred cell doors. They then covered the exterior of the cells with a wall of thick stone. Consequently, there was a space between the iron cell walls and the stone walls of about six inches. Over the years, items that disappeared into this space had proven to be irretrievable. While our construction workers were removing the old cell block they would at times come across a variety of items from the old days that had fallen into this narrow space. It was a bit like a time capsule that revealed old newspapers, whiskey bottles, clothing, and pieces of china.

One day, one of the workers came up to me and handed me a book he found in the space. It was the Colorado Statutes of 1908. All the laws of the state fit in one volume. Murder, rape, assault, stealing, and trespassing were all against the law in 1908. Although that time was not entirely peaceful, I think research would show it was an era in which people were free to walk around most towns and cities without fear.

Today, Colorado has over 30,000 laws filling twelve volumes that stack up about four feet high. And of course, predictably, lawlessness is commonplace, even in vogue. Most of the laws and regulations

> "Hold all of our people personally accountable for their ACTIONS through the criminal justice system. If someone burglarizes a house... [or] drives a motor vehicle under the influence of alcohol, cocaine, or marijuana, he or she must be held accountable."
>
> —Judge James P. Gray
> **Why Our Drug Laws Have Failed And What We Can Do About It**, page 12

cannot be understood, and because of their sheer numbers they cannot possibly be enforced.

There are 600 traffic laws alone. Think about that when you drive to work tomorrow. And even with all these laws, some people still drive like fools.

Our tax code is 500 times the size of the Constitution. It is so convoluted no one—not the courts, juries, or IRS agents—no one can tell you without some doubt what it all means. One agent told me that in some jurisdictions up to 50 percent of the people are just not filing any tax returns. They are living completely outside the system. Now, the biggest tax cheat of the century gets a pardon. Does all this make you feel like a chump when you write those checks to the government?

It appears to me the more broken the system, the more laws are passed to try to correct its deficiencies, but in fact the problem is the number of laws itself.

The Colorado Bureau of Investigation announced last year the Colorado Instant Check System stopped over 90 convicted murders from purchasing firearms from licensed dealers in Colorado.

THE MORE BROKEN THE SYSTEM, THE MORE LAWS ARE PASSED TO TRY TO CORRECT THE DEFICIENCIES, BUT IN FACT THE PROBLEM IS THE NUMBER OF LAWS ITSELF.

As a peace officer, I think it is good these murderers are denied the ability to purchase firearms. But in our efforts to correct one problem, murderers having firearms, we fail to recognize and address a much more fundamental problem. That being, of course, why in the hell are there 90 convicted murderers out walking around on the streets of Colorado?

This extreme number of laws has blurred the criminal justice system's response in upholding them. Trying to identify the laws that are important becomes a nightmare for all involved in the system. Officers are required to carry around volumes of peace officer's manuals, law books, code books, and policy and procedures manuals—all in an effort to perform a job that used to be done with a little bit of common sense.

The Bible tells us Moses walked up Mount Sinai and came down with 10 laws to live by, most of them about one sentence long. Moses' four words, "Thou shall not steal," are now Colorado Revised Statutes 18-4-401 through 18-4-416. It is over 24,000 words long, and if you really don't want to be a victim of theft you still need a car alarm, house alarm, 25 keys and a digital credit card.

Governor Johnson of New Mexico has a story he tells about an ancient city-state in Greece. This city-state practiced true democracy and allowed any citizen to propose a law to the council of all citizens who met on occasion in a large coliseum. The one restriction on proposed laws was that the citizen proposing a new law had to stand

> "Opium and morphine are certainly dangerous, habit-forming drugs. But once the principle is admitted that it is the duty of government to protect the individual from his own foolishness, no serious objection can be raised against further encroachments..."
>
> —Ludwig von Mises, Economist
> Human Action, 1949

on a scaffold with a noose about his neck while the law was being debated and voted on. If the citizens voted the proposed new law down as being unnecessary, the citizen proposing the law was immediately hanged.

Moses and the ancient Greeks were onto something we have forgotten. Pass only the laws that are really necessary. Keep them few in number, and make them easy enough for a child to read and understand. If we took this simple advice to heart, we would find new respect for, and honor in, our government and its institutions.

Doc Shores

I have a book in my office that was given to me by a friend in Telluride who collects old books. The book was written by Sheriff Doc Shores of Gunnison County; it's called *Memoirs of a Lawman*. Doc was the sheriff in Gunnison from 1890 to 1900. His book is the fascinating story of his life as a sheriff in that era on the Western Slope of Colorado.

Doc tells a story about how he became sheriff. One day, when he was on Main Street in Gunnison, he heard a number of gunshots. He turned and saw a couple of young punks riding down the street on horseback shooting wildly. A shopkeeper stepped out of his store to see what the commotion was about and was shot dead by the punks as they rode by.

Doc immediately grabbed his rifle, got on his horse and gave chase. In the ensuing gun battle Doc was able to capture the outlaws, and the people of Gunnison recognized him as a hero and elected him sheriff.

If you did the same thing today you would be labeled a nut case, if not arrested.

In another account, Doc recalls investigating a train robbery near Salida. Doc and that famous lawman (and sometimes outlaw) Tom Horn were given the job of capturing the train robbers. They arrived at the scene of the crime about three days after the event to find the tracks of the two horsemen they believed to be the outlaws. They took off at once to follow the tracks.

It was a slow trek through the mountains, following tracks one at a time. After a few days they came across some people on the trail who told them they had seen the robbers heading south about a week earlier. Knowing they were on the right trail, the two lawmen sped up a bit in an attempt to overtake the outlaws, who were a full seven days ahead of them. As they continued their ride following the tracks, they slept at night outside in the mountains with nothing more than a blanket to cover themselves. They dug in the soil around abandoned homesteads looking for spuds to eat. They rode 14 hours or more every day in the saddle.

They followed the tracks for 43 days, through southern Colorado, into New Mexico and then Texas, where they finally overtook the two outlaws. Without backup, bulletproof vests, automatic rifles, or fire trucks to hide behind (like police had at Columbine), Doc and Tom Horn apprehended the two armed and desperate outlaws and then turned around and brought them back to justice in Colorado.

I tell you those two stories about Doc because it demonstrates to me what a true citizen of a republic should be. One cannot tell

> "Prohibition will work great injury to the cause of temperance. It is a species of intemperance within itself, for it goes beyond the bounds of reason in that it attempts to control a man's appetite by legislation and makes a crime out of things that are not crimes. A prohibition law strikes at the very principle upon which our Government was founded."
>
> —Abraham Lincoln, Republican President

the difference in the actions between Doc the citizen, who is always prepared to defend his community, rising to the challenge and fearlessly chasing the murdering punks, or Doc the sheriff, who bravely never gives up on the trail of the outlaws. Both citizen and sheriff, Doc knows his duty.

I want all citizens to be prepared to stand up, even if in voice only, to enforce the principles of liberty and responsibility. One does not exist without the other. Let us regain our lost responsibilities of educating our children, providing for our families, and defending ourselves.

Keep in mind, and in your heart, the words of Thomas Jefferson, the symbol of American liberty to the world:

> *"A wise and frugal Government, which shall restrain men from injuring one another, shall leave them otherwise free to regulate their own pursuits of industry and improvement, and shall not take from the mouth of labor the bread it [has] earned. This is the sum of good government."*

Enforce the Bill of Rights

Good news? Attorney General John Ashcroft said he is now going to support the Constitution. What about the Ninth and Tenth Amendments?

> *"The enumeration in the Constitution of certain rights shall not be construed to deny or disparage others retained by the people."*
> — *Ninth Amendment of the Bill of Rights*

> *"The powers not delegated to the United States by the Constitution, nor prohibited by it to the States, are reserved to the States respectively, or to the people."*
> —*Tenth Amendment of the Bill of Rights*

Why is Ashcroft fighting medical marijuana after the people in many states voted for it? Why is he supporting increased federal law enforcement? Why does the justice department need 700 new ATF agents and federal lawyers to enforce existing gun laws?

When he talks about the right of "law-abiding" citizens to keep firearms, what laws is he talking about? All of them?

Remember there are over 30,000 laws in Colorado alone. The number of federal laws is obscene. That "law-abiding" stuff sounds pretty good until you remember that they were only "enforcing the federal laws on the books" at both Ruby Ridge and Waco.

Of course now the Supreme Court allows cops to drag seemingly "law-abiding" citizens away in handcuffs for not wearing their seat belts. Do you get charged with "committing a crime while in possession of a firearm" if you take off your seat belt and you have a rifle in your truck? Don't laugh: some cop or federal agent might try it, especially if you are a bit "off," such as if you're a member of some weird church or you have dancing bear stickers in the windows.

A real Attorney General would say, "We are going to cut the Justice Department in half. We are going to expect the states to do their jobs and control 'firearm violence' by enforcing their own laws against murder, assault, and armed robbery.

> "The naive advocates of government interference with consumption... unwittingly support the cause of censorship, inquisition, intolerance, and the persecution of dissenters."
>
> —Ludwig von Mises, Economist
> Human Action, 1949

"I am going to file suits against any town, city, or state that passes laws which violate the people's basic right to defend themselves, to choose what is best for their bodies, or to decide whom to pray to."

Sheriff Bill Masters

The Trouble with Seat Belt Laws

28-year-old Trooper Randall Vetter clung to life for five days after he was shot in the head with a rifle bullet. The Texas officer was married, and he was father to an 8-month-old child. He had been shot, but not by drug gangs, bank robbers, or escaped convicts. He was shot and killed by Melvin Hale, a retired 72-year-old rancher who had never been in serious trouble with the law before.

Trooper Vetter had stopped Mr. Hale for not wearing his seat belt as required by Texas law. After the 6' 7" trooper got Mr. Hale's driver's license, he returned to his patrol car to write a $25.00 citation. Mr. Hale then got out of his truck armed with an assault-style rifle and shot Trooper Vetter through the windshield of the patrol car, fatally injuring him.

Melvin Hale then reached into the patrol car and used the wounded Trooper's radio to report the incident to the police dispatcher. He calmly waited for other officers to arrive, who arrested him without incident. Mr. Hale readily admitted to shooting Trooper Vetter.

"I did it," he told a group of reporters. "I'm a law-abiding citizen. I like to drive down the road without being arrested."

In his concern about being a law-abiding citizen, Mr. Hale must have missed the one that prohibits shooting people.

Senior Journal claimed shortly after the shooting that Mr. Hale's actions must be because of dementia or Alzheimer's. I would guess that Mr. Hale's attorneys will agree.

It was reported that Mr. Hale contributed to both the Texas State Troopers Association Officers' Memorial Fund and the Deputy Sheriff's Association a week before the shooting. In addition, he had a "Support Your Local Sheriff" bumper sticker in his kitchen. It sounds like a case of dementia. Or is it?

Unknown to Trooper Vetter, Mr. Hale, although he had never been arrested before, had a history of complaining about laws, especially the seat belt law. One trooper, after an encounter with Mr. Hale a few months before the shooting, wrote a memo to all officers in the county advising caution and warning them of Hale's strong opposition to the seat belt law. Sadly, the memo never made it to Trooper Vetter's attention.

Three years before Mr. Hale shot Trooper Vetter, and 54 miles to the south, Gail Atwater was driving in her car with her two kids. Her 4-year-old son had a small plastic toy bat that was attached by a suction cup to one of the car windows. While driving down a residential street near her home, the plastic bat fell off the window. As is typical of children, her son was upset about the loss of his favorite toy and he worried it would be run over. Everyone with kids knows the drill: you have to go look for it.

> "If you want a Big Brother, you get all that comes with it."
>
> —Erich Fromm

Mrs. Atwater turned around and started slowly driving up the quiet street looking for the lost bat. She allowed the kids to take off their seat belts so they could look out the windows to help with the search. She was driving about 15 mph.

At that time Officer Bart Turek of the Largo Vista Police Department came around the corner driving a patrol car. Seeing Mrs. Atwater and her children with no seat belts on, he motioned for her to stop her car.

Sheriff Bill Masters

Officer Turek had stopped Mrs. Atwater once before, mistakenly thinking her son had not been wearing a seat belt. On that previous occasion, Officer Turek saw the boy was in fact securely fastened in, so he acknowledged his error and let her go. But on this day the soccer mom was going to jail.

Mrs. Atwater later reported that Officer Turek came up and jabbed his finger at her window and yelled, "You are going to jail!" According to Atwater, the officer continued to berate her and she finally asked him to lower his voice because her children were becoming frightened by his actions. That, she claimed, made the officer yell even louder. He then asked to see her driver's license, which she said she didn't have because her purse had been stolen earlier in the week. Officer Turek replied, "I have heard that 200 times." I'm sure his estimate was low.

When Mrs. Atwater realized she faced arrest, she asked if she could take her children home first, so they wouldn't be terrified by going with her to the jail. One of Mrs. Atwater's friends happened to drive by at that point and agreed to take the children. Presumably they wore their seat belts.

Mrs. Atwater was handcuffed, placed in the back of the patrol car, and driven—without a seat belt—to the jail. Her car was impounded. At the jail, officers removed her shoes, eyeglasses, and jewelry; took a mug shot; then placed her in a cell for an hour. She was then allowed to post a $300 bail bond, so she was released.

Mrs. Atwater later went to court and pled guilty to the charge of not wearing a seat belt. She paid the fine of $50.00. She also sued the City of Largo Vista for violating her Fourth Amendment protections against unreasonable seizures.

To most Americans, the actions of the Largo Vista police officer seem unreasonable. Certainly the officer could have stopped Mrs. Atwater, counseled her about driving without her seat belt, and even given her a ticket if he thought the violation required one. Some officers I know would have ignored the whole issue and helped her look for the toy bat.

Mrs. Atwater's attorneys argued that police should distinguish between laws that are very serious and those that are less serious. They said the police should not arrest people for committing crimes that do not reach the level of "breaches of the peace" or crimes that are close to some form of violence.

The majority of the Supreme Court decided against Mrs. Atwater, stating that historically police have been allowed to arrest people for less serious crimes. The Court stated that peace officers, both before and after the founding of our country, arrested people for such crimes as breaking the Sabbath, being a vagabond, night-walking, and performing "crafty science."

> "All laws must be objective (and objectively justifiable): men must know clearly, and in advance of taking an action, what the law forbids them to do (and why), what constitutes a crime and what penalty they will incur if they commit it."
>
> —Ayn Rand
> **The Nature of Government**

I must admit that, while many of my friends commit those older crimes on a regular basis, they all drive with their seat belts fastened. However, the penalties for performing "crafty science" were quite a bit more severe in places like Salem, Massachusetts, in the 1600s than driving without your seat belt is in rural Texas today. My guess is that without physical detention, few people would voluntarily show up to take their place burning at the stake.

The Court, in defending officers' rights to arrest people for minor offenses punishable by nothing more than a fine, stated: "We cannot expect every police officer to know the details of frequently complex penalty schemes." The Court added, "Officers in the field frequently have neither the time nor competency to determine the severity of the offense for which they are considering arresting a person."

Basically the court is saying that the laws are too complicated for officers to understand. But forget the officers for a minute: what about the citizens?

I HAVE SOME IMPORTANT NEWS FOR THE... HIGH COURT: NOBODY... HAS THE TIME OR COMPETENCY TO UNDER-STAND THE LAWS OR THE "COMPLEX PENALTY SCHEMES."

I have some important news for the Justices of the High Court: nobody, not the officers, the courts, the legislatures, or—most importantly—the citizens, has the time or competency to understand the laws or the "complex penalty schemes."

I agree with the Supreme Court: officers should have the right to arrest people who violate the law, any law. But that is not the problem. The problem is, the laws often interfere with adult behavior that can hurt no one but the offender. Of course the legislatures must pass "complex penalty schemes" for minor violations. The intrusiveness of the laws, along with the need to hand light sentences to first-time offenders, demands excessive complexity.

Somewhere along the line our legislators got the idea that if they don't pass any new laws to protect people from themselves, or better yet, to "save the children," they're not doing their jobs. In fact, most often the job of legislators should be not to pass new laws, but to protect the rights of citizens to take care of themselves and their families.

Having been in public office for my entire adult life, I can understand where most Senators and Representatives are coming from. When some do-gooder is in your face wanting protection from some imagined evil, it's hard for an elected official to say there is nothing he or she can or should do. The noblest and bravest thing an elected official can do for a citizen is say, "I am not going to help you on this one. Your request is outside the limits of what a responsible and limited government should be concerned with."

Once a Colorado legislator introduced a law that would prohibit dogs from riding in the back of pickup trucks. Some constituent of hers had called and expressed concern about a dog riding in the back of a truck, out in the cold and wind. And with no seat belt on, the poor thing.

Any reasonable person would have told the constituent to get a life. Better yet, the legislator should have said, "Look, I am not going to waste the taxpayers' money to pass a law for this. Ultimately, each new law brings with it the threat of putting citizens in jail. Police have to be paid to enforce the law. I'm not going to ask state troopers to put their lives on the line because they have to tell some crazy old coot with a rifle he can't put his dog in the back of his pickup truck."

> "One of the main psychological, ethical underpinnings of libertarianism is the premise that we must take responsibility for our own lives and be accountable for our own actions. There is no other way for a civilized society to operate."
>
> **— Nathaniel Branden**
> **The Foundations of a Free Society**
> http://www.nathanielbranden.net/ess/ess02.html

Legislators need to remember that after they pass a law, any law, the police can arrest the violators, strip-search them, and place them in jail. If the violator resists, the police can beat them, stun-gun them, tear-gas them, seize their property, and shoot them.

Sheriff Bill Masters

No matter how "helpful" the law is or how "safe it will make you," some people will violate the law just because they are adults, they aren't hurting or endangering anyone else, and they want to thumb their noses at the law, at lawmen, and at the government. It's the American way.

I'm sure Trooper Vetter was a well-trained and brave police officer, one willing to take on all the dangerous crooks of the day. Like most officers, he would have rushed to the scene of a bank robbery or shooting, while everyone else was running away. But the proud "Lone Star State" legislature let him down. Instead of looking for crooks, stolen cars, bank robbers, murderers, or kidnapped children, Texas lawmen, along with the rest of us, have been turned into nothing more than regulators on the constant prowl for retired ranchers and housewives who don't want to wear their seat belts.

Why I'm a Libertarian

I am really proud to be an American. We don't say that often enough today. I thought of this when I was watching the news and they were interviewing one of the former directors of the CIA. They were talking about the FBI agent who was a spy for the Russians for 15 years. The reporter was questioning the director about how we could prevent similar incidents in the future—should they use polygraphs on all the agents, better background investigations, and different investigative techniques?

And the director had an interesting response. He said the best defense against these kinds of spies is to have spies in the foreign service of our enemy's government. In that way, foreigners who are spying for the United States could tell us when our adversaries have spies in our government.

He went on to say that American traitors, like this FBI agent, who spy on our country usually do so for money and seldom do it for philosophical reasons, whereas the foreigners who volunteer to spy for the U.S. on their governments usually do so out of a philosophical belief that the principles the United States represents are superior to those of the government of their homeland.

He then stated, and this is the important part, "Thomas Jefferson is still our best recruiter."

From Tienanmen Square to Cuba, freedom fighters quote Jefferson in their own language. Sadly, sometimes Jefferson's own country, our country, fails to live up to their expectations.

This is the core belief of the Libertarian movement: people must embrace liberty and at the same time take responsibility, completely and totally, for their actions. You cannot have liberty for long if you fail to accept the corresponding virtue of responsibility.

> "[D]isclosures of a quiet relationship between Amtrak and the federal Drug Enforcement Agency to share the proceeds of cash seized from travelers have alarmed civil libertarians and outraged some defense attorneys."
>
> —Greg Land
> Creating Loafing Atlanta, July 18, 2001

We must not abdicate our responsibility and surrender it to the government. It is our responsibility to deal with such issues as health care, our retirement, raising and educating our children, the defense of our homes and families, our domestic relations, and our own alcohol or drug abuse. If we fail to take responsibility for our own lives, we can blame only ourselves when the government takes away our liberty to determine how those issues will be addressed.

Sheriff Bill Masters

We can draw a comparison to management strategies in the business world. A person with the responsibility for a problem must also have the authority to make decisions necessary to deal with the job.

As a nation, as a people, we are slowly but continually giving up more of our authority and responsibility to the government so we can sit back and be less burdened by our duties as parents of children, and as citizens of a republic.

Many people ask me, "Are Libertarians conservative or liberal?" We are neither. Some of our ideas seem liberal because we defend civil rights. Others appear conservative because we advocate a free market and believe businesses are over-regulated and over-taxed.

What do we stand for?

• Libertarians seek to repeal the failed policy of drug prohibition.

For the past 40 years we have waged an escalating war on drugs. And each year the problem has gotten worse. It started out in the early Sixties as an inner city problem with a little bit of marijuana. We now have cocaine, heroin, methamphetamine, ecstasy—you name it. Drugs are now available in every government school and in every town, village, and prison.

Charged with an impossible task, police are more and more aggressive at fighting drugs. Law enforcement and military agents in this war mistakenly kill increasing numbers of innocent people. Remember Veronica and Charity Bowers, the Baptist missionaries. Remember Zeke Hernandez, the young goat herder.

Whenever some gains are made against one drug, like a limit on the supply of cocaine, people turn to manufacturing other drugs like methamphetamine, which they can make in their own homes from supplies purchased at Wal-mart.

Last year we arrested 700,000 American citizens for possession of marijuana at a phenomenal cost of time, manpower and money. These arrests alone placed an incredible burden on law enforcement, jails, and the courts. The drug war has taken precious criminal justice resources away from tracking down and punishing killers, rapists, child molesters, thieves, and other real criminals.

What is the Libertarian alternative? First, we must hold people responsible for their direct actions that endanger or harm people or their property. This must be the concentrated focus of all police, criminal courts and punishment resources.

Further, if we continue to allow drug addiction or alcoholism as an excuse for criminal behavior, we will never solve the problem. I don't care what anyone says, drug use and alcoholism are choices made by free-willed individuals. Criminal behavior needs to be judged, and perpetrators need to be held responsible for their actions.

> "[W]e cannot incarcerate our way out of the drug problem."
>
> --Nadine Strossen,
> American Civil Liberties Union

Next, we need to allow drug users to purchase drugs through legitimate medical centers. This will destroy overnight the profit in the criminal drug cartels, now estimated to be at $200 billion per year. Drug-dealing gangs will be nonexistent, dangerous meth labs unnecessary, and peace can return to our cities and our borders. Addicts won't need to sell drugs to children or steal to support their habit. Drug enforcement agents can return to the task of finding missing or exploited children and solving other crimes with direct victims. Jails and prisons will have enough beds so that murderers and child abusers can spend their life behind bars rather then be paroled, due to lack of space.

• Libertarians want simpler, lower taxes.

Our tax code is now 500 times the size of our Constitution. It is so confusing and convoluted that no one, not tax attorneys, judges, IRS agents, or accountants, knows with any degree of certainty what it all means.

A recent study by the Treasury department revealed that 47 percent of the time, the IRS' own agents answered taxpayers' questions incorrectly. And remember, if you follow the incorrect advice, you are still liable for all taxes, interest and penalties, even those which accrue as a direct result of the erroneous information.

In some jurisdictions up to 50 percent of the people are not filing any tax returns. Almost 2,000 citizens who filed tax returns last year with a reported income of over $200,000 are paying no taxes at all, due to clever manipulations of tax shelters.

If you ask your Republican or Democratic representatives, they will all agree the IRS is out of control, and that reform is needed in that agency. But that's not the problem. Congress passes these outrageous laws, endorses the regulations, and funds the collection agency, but when a citizen complains about it, the politicians blame the bureaucracy they created, as if they can do nothing else.

Libertarians know that money is needed to run a government; we must have a system of fundraising. But the current monstrosity should be replaced by a fair, simple tax code with low rates. Americans deserve a new tax code no more than a few sentences long, a code the simplest among us can understand and respect because of its fundamental fairness.

• Libertarians believe in a strong national defense.

Our sons and daughters should never be sacrificed without a clear declaration of war, as our Constitution requires.

If we follow our Constitution, our military men and women will know the public is behind them in a fight that truly involves our national interest. Our solders, airmen, sailors, and Marines are not the world's police officers; they are not some New World Order army led by foreign commanders. They are our children. They serve to protect our country.

While we send out our military to patrol the world or eradicate coca crops in South America, we leave ourselves increasingly defenseless against missile attack by foreign tyrants. FDR, in his "Day of Infamy" speech regarding the sudden surprise attack on Pearl Harbor by the Japanese empire, stated, "We will make ever certain that this form of treachery shall never endanger us again." Those words have been forgotten.

> "Politicians never accuse you of 'greed' for wanting other people's money—only for wanting to keep your own money."
>
> —Joseph Sobran

Without a doubt, we are on the road to great suffering due to our misallocation of military resources.

Libertarians believe a true defense starts with the protection of our homeland. We must change our priorities from the hopeless task of world peacekeeping to protecting our country from sudden and deliberate attack.

Sheriff Bill Masters

Libertarians support limited government and individual rights and responsibilities. In short, we seek to restore the vision of good government outlined by Thomas Jefferson.

Libertarians support strong families. We want to limit government spending so we can return to a day when both parents don't have to work almost five months out of the year just to support our government. Rather than spending their time and energy working for the government, fathers and mothers should have more time to counsel and supervise their children. I believe this alone will go a long way toward solving many of our juvenile crime and drug problems.

Speak to your Republican or Democratic representatives, as I have, about the number of laws or how complex they are, and they all will agree with you. Then they will return to the state house to pass more laws so confusing that armies of attorneys and judges will argue over their meaning for years to come.

LIBERTARIANS SUPPORT LAWS NECESSARY TO RESTRAIN MEN FROM INJURING ONE ANOTHER... LAWS SHOULD BE FEW IN NUMBER AND SIMPLE ENOUGH FOR A CHILD TO READ...

The sheer volume of laws makes the fair or effective enforcement of any of them extremely difficult. Many laws contradict one another. Others require police officers and judges to apply complex laws to simple issues as opposed to using common sense to solve the problem.

One of my kids asked me, "I know that ignorance of the law is no excuse, but what if you are just plain ignorant?"

I had some prisoners in court not long ago. The judge was passing the required legal sentence on one fellow, who had wrongly driven after drinking:

"Five days in jail, $136.50 in fines and costs, $16.75 to the victims' compensation fund, 120 hours of useful public service. Defendant must meet with alcohol evaluator within one month and complete level one and two alcohol training, probation for one year, status hearing on September 18th. Violation of any condition will result in a warrant for defendant's arrest."

The poor guy scratched his head and turned to me, "Sheriff, I got the five days in jail part, but what was the rest of that stuff?" He will never make his probation. Instead, he will be returned to the system over and over again because it is just too complicated for him to follow.

My small county has over 300 active arrest warrants, and most of them are not issued because the person committed a crime. Most warrants are issued for people who just couldn't comply with sentences, which order them to jump through a series of nonsensical hoops they can neither see nor understand.

Many of us can hire attorneys to help us through legal minefields, but the poor, the simple, or those with limited language skills are often left languishing in jail because they fail to comprehend an increasingly complex system.

> "We fight not to enslave, but to set a country free, and to make room upon the earth for honest men to live in... Those who expect to reap the blessings of freedom, must... undergo the fatigues of supporting it."
>
> —Thomas Paine

Libertarians support laws necessary to restrain men from injuring one another and to maintain order. These laws should be few in number and simple enough for a child to read and understand. If we took this simple plan to heart, we would find new respect for, and honor in, our government and its institutions.

Sheriff Bill Masters

Libertarians believe in people. Unfortunately, many government agents want to be like fathers, telling citizens what to do or what not to do. Others in government want to act like mothers and wipe our noses or make us wear a jacket when it's cold outside. A Libertarian government will treat people like adults. We will guarantee to each person the liberty and responsibility independent citizens must possess to keep our republic free and strong.

Appendix A

Telluride Sheriff
Just Says No to the Drug War

by Nancy Lofholm

Denver Post
August 28, 2000

Sheriff Bill Masters

Telluride Sheriff Just Says No to the Drug War

By Nancy Lofholm, Denver Post Western Slope Bureau
Reprinted with permission.

TELLURIDE—When Bill Masters was just a little towheaded shaver growing up in Los Angeles, he had a curious habit that signaled where he was going in life.

Crossing streets, he would clutch his mother with one hand and direct traffic with the other.

Some 45 years later, he still puzzles about this. He grew up in a family of academics, not cops.

But law enforcement drew Masters and turned him into a county sheriff who breaks out of the box—a sheriff who thinks, and more importantly says, that the war on drugs is ludicrous, the criminal justice system is a farce and the law-making arm of the government has run amok.

Masters' philosophy has played well in San Miguel County and its famous county seat of Telluride, a town that has gone from hard-working, hard-playing mining burg to chic playground-of-the-rich resort in the 25 years Masters has been in law enforcement here.

He is now in his fifth term as sheriff. He has the distinction of being the nation's only registered Libertarian Party sheriff.

And he holds the highest elected office among Colorado Libertarians.

Since he "came out" as a libertarian candidate in the 1998 election after previously having to run as a Republican to be included on the ballot, his popularity has only grown. He won with 80 percent of the vote, his largest margin ever.

Masters, who favors Hawaiian shirts over staid uniforms, doesn't order people to obey Colorado's 33,000 laws—many of which he believes are unnecessary. His message instead is that citizens be responsible.

Excuses such as "alcohol made me do it" won't fly in his county, where violent crime falls well below the national norm and the average sheriff's log is made up of motorist troubles, illegal campfires and burglaries.

"Libertarians say there is no excuse if you hurt someone or their property. You have to be held accountable," said the 49-year-old Masters, a Libertarian for half his life.

Masters extends that gospel of personal responsibility to victims.

In a "message from the sheriff" printed on the back of a victims' rights pamphlet, Masters tells citizens of his county: "It is your responsibility to protect yourself and your family from criminals. If you rely on the government for protection, you are going to be at least disappointed and at worst injured or killed."

The one area of the law that really sets Masters apart—the subject that spurs him to wave his arms and roll his desk chair back and forth to punctuate important points—is drugs.

When he was first appointed and later elected sheriff in the late 1970s, Masters said he wanted to prove he could be tough on drugs. He helped bust the former town marshal, a former town board member and a number of well-known citizens. He even received a framed certificate of appreciation from the Drug Enforcement

> "God grant that not only the love of liberty but a thorough knowledge of the rights of man may pervade all the nations of the earth, so that a philosopher may set his foot anywhere on its surface and say: 'This is my country.'"
> —Benjamin Franklin

Sheriff Bill Masters

Administration that now hangs on a wall of his spare office along with a quote from Thomas Jefferson, the poem "If," and a small sign advising his employees to GOYAKOD (get off your a— and knock on doors).

"Just look at how much good those arrests did," Masters said with a wry laugh. "We spend $50 billion a year on drug enforcement in this country, and we let pedophiles and murderers out of prison because there is not enough room. The prisons are full of drug users."

Masters said a number of other Colorado sheriffs have told him in private that they agree with his drug stance. But they won't say it publicly. If they did, they might not be re-elected.

Pitkin County Sheriff Bob Braudis is one of the few openly in Masters' corner.

"I share his philosophy. If you have a drug problem you should go to the doctor, not to jail," Braudis said. "Bill has let that genie out of the bottle and not suffered politically for it. He has an awful lot of courage for stating this."

Ron Crickenberger, national political director of the Libertarian Party, said Masters has become a "shining example" for other Libertarians across America who are considering running for law enforcement positions while openly opposing drug laws.

Masters spoke about that stance when he addressed the National Libertarian Convention in June.

He told convention attendees a story about a trip he made to the FBI training academy in Quantico, Va., several years ago.

He said he was brokenhearted to find the academy swarming with bright, enthusiastic young agents-in-training for the DEA but only a handful of older, overworked agents assigned to a case dealing with suspected child abductions by a serial killer.

Masters, a man known for his infectious giggle, doesn't try to hide the tears running down one cheek when he repeats the story in his office.

He had gone to Quantico for help with the case of a young Montrose woman whose murdered body was found in his county two years after she was abducted from a Montrose parking lot.

The Buffy Rice Donohue murder case is one that Masters, a father of four, has refused to let die even after other law enforcement officials have washed their hands of it.

The man believed to have killed Donohue is facing a death sentence in two other murders and has never been prosecuted for Donohue's murder. His former girlfriend, whom Masters said he believes was an accomplice in the murder, has been sentenced only for being an accessory.

Masters is continuing to investigate to bring some overdue justice in Donohue's murder.

He showed the same dogged determination in the 1990 murder of Eva Berg Shoen, a resident of the Telluride Ski Ranches. It took five years of meticulous investigative work to arrest and convict a New Mexico man for the slaying.

> "Liberty is the only thing you cannot have unless you are willing to give it to others."
>
> —William Allen White

Masters said solving that case was possible because his deputies were able to focus on the crime because they didn't have to spend half their time chasing after drug dealers. He also said that he doesn't allow them to spend their time on "touchy-feely" extra programs such as drug education in schools.

Jill Masters, who worked as a sheriff's investigator before marrying Bill Masters 10 years ago, said she doesn't view what her husband is doing as radical.

"It's actually old-fashioned. It's the way law enforcement used to be practiced," she said.

But Braudis said he expects Masters to be recognized someday as "an early pioneer" for his cutting-edge stance on the drug war.

Crickenberger said he expects even more.

"I would certainly like to see Bill run for a higher office—for state representative or Congress," Crickenberger said. "We will be encouraging him to do so."

Appendix B

A Brief History
of the Drug War

by Stephen Raher

Originally published as "Why Are So Many
Drug Addicts in Prison?" by Stephen Raher
in *Prison Policy News*, vol. 1, no. 5. Reprinted
with permission of Epimethian Press.
Copyright (C) 2000 Epimethian Press.

Epimethian Press&Distribution
P.O. Box 2143
Colorado Springs, CO 80901
info@epimethian.org

Sheriff Bill Masters

IT IS HARD TO IMAGINE a resident of the United States who has not heard of the "War on Drugs." Recognized widely (but not unanimously) as a failure, the drug war depends on incarcerating staggering numbers of people in an attempt to curb illegal drug use. The current reliance on incarceration is fraught with problems—high costs, lack of treatment resources, and the impact on communities, to name a few.

One notable result of the growing prison population is a change in the nature of prison overcrowding. While prison overcrowding used to take the form of too many inmates in outdated facilities, the current trend centers around systems that are too big to support. What was recently an overcrowding problem (with state prisons at 115% of capacity in 1995) has become a building problem (as in "building too much").

Statistics from the most recent year available (1999) show that for the first time in years, a majority of state prison systems are operating at or below capacity. On a national basis, prisons exceed capacity by only 1%. Despite less crowded prisons the U.S. now incarcerates over two million people (US BJS "Prisoners"). Some activists regard the study of drug war history to be a largely academic activity, with no application to building an opposition movement. I object to this belief, since the U.S. attitude towards drug control was born out of a popular movement and has been continuously shaped by such movements. In order to thoroughly understand the nature of the drug war and formulate ideas on how to challenge it, a brief history is quite useful.

Early History

Use of drugs such as opium, morphine, and their derivatives was quite commonplace in nineteenth century America. While most students of contemporary high school drug education programs know about the use of coca leaves in early Coca-Cola and the opium trade with China, the matter of drug addiction at the turn of the century is much more extensive than usually acknowledged. It is estimated that by 1900 there were somewhere in the neighborhood of 250,000 regular users of addictive drugs in the U.S.

While this number may seem large (taking into consideration the smaller population of the country in 1900 as compared to today), it is actually surprisingly small considering that such drugs were available over the counter. Cocaine, morphine, laudanum, and heroin were all available in drug stores and through the mail. Until the Pure Food and Drug Act of 1906, products containing such ingredients did not even need to list them on the label (Musto 1-5).

Taking into account the disproportionate impact of the contemporary Drug War on racial minorities in the U.S., it is particularly noteworthy that the origins of drug control were rooted in overt racism. Anti-drug crusaders of the early twentieth century spoke not only of the general "moral" destruction caused by drugs, but also capitalized on Southern fear of African-Americans and Western fears of Chinese immigrants. Crusader Dr. Hamilton Wright urged Congress to pass harsh drug laws, stating that "it has been authoritatively stated that cocaine is often the direct incentive to the crime of rape by the Negroes of the South and other sections of the

> "The path you propose of more police, more jails, use of the military in foreign countries, harsh penalties for drug users, and a whole panoply of repressive measures can only make a bad situation worse. The drug war cannot be won by those tactics without undermining the human liberty and individual freedom that you and I cherish."
>
> —Milton Friedman, Open Letter to Bill Bennett

country"; still other rhetoric warned that the effects of drugs "make Negro cocaine users 'oblivious of their prescribed bounds' and... lead them to 'attack white society'" (Bertram, et al. 64-66).

In 1902 the American Federation of Labor mounted a campaign which stated that "Chinese opium smokers had spread the 'deathly habit' to 'hundreds, aye thousands, of our American boys and girls'" (Bertram, et al. 64). By the early 1900s many people were concerned by the growing use of drugs in the U.S., and the medical community quickly rose to defend the proper use of drugs against the zeal of prohibitionists. Thus the battle lines were drawn between the medical community (advocating a treatment-based approach) and reformers (advocating a punitive-based prohibition).

The first major legislation to forge a compromise between doctors and reformers was the District of Columbia Pharmacy Act of 1906. Since federal control of the drug trade had not been clearly established, Congress passed a law that applied only to the Congressionally-controlled seat of the national government. The Act established procedures for prescriptions and registered pharmacists. While this legislation had limited scope, it was held up as a model for narcotic drug reform (Musto 21-22).

By December of 1914, concern over drug use was substantial enough that a stronger (yet still relatively mild) attempt to curb drug addiction surfaced and was passed by Congress in the form of the Harrison Narcotics Act of 1914. There was certainly domestic concern and outrage on the part of the general public, and many politicians supported these sentiments; however, the factor that finally made passage of a narcotics bill possible actually originated on the international stage. The U.S. realized the multinational nature of the drug trade early on and—despite isolationist tendencies in the U.S. government—signed on to several international conventions agreeing to fight the drug trade (Boggress).

Now that the U.S. was party to these conventions, the country needed to comply with the spirit of them, and as a result, the Department of State proposed the Harrison bill. It should be noted that the Harrison Act looked quite different from today's Drug War. The aim was to control dispersal of drugs, not criminalize users. The specter of a federal drug police force made many politicians uneasy. The most significant opposition to the bill in Congress came from southern Democrats who feared that federal control of narcotics would lead to state police powers being assumed by the federal government.

As a result the Harrison Act made the issue into one of taxation. The Act simply required that producers and distributors of drugs register with the Treasury Department, keep records of their transactions, and pay taxes on the drugs. In order to obtain narcotics, the Act required citizens to obtain "a prescription from a physician who 'prescribed [it] in good faith' and did so 'in the pursuit of his professional practice only'"

> "[T]he only sane course now open is to end the Drug War and restore complete medical liberty, totally and overnight..."
>
> —Vin Suprynowicz, Syndicated Columnist
> Send In the Waco Killers, page 65

(Bertram, et al. 67-68). It is noteworthy, however, that a scant four years after passage of the Act, the U.S. government itself argued before the Supreme Court that "Congress gave [the Harrison Act] the appearance of a taxing measure in order to give it a coating of constitutionality, but that it really was a police measure" (U.S. v. Jin Fuey Moy at 401).

The original intent of the legislation was to target irresponsible producers and vendors, not to criminalize drug users. How, then, did the tide shift? Partly it was thanks to societal changes, but the Supreme Court paved the way in the second decade of the twentieth century. Immediately after the act took effect, the Treasury Department waged a campaign to expand their powers (Bertram, et al. 69-71), and courts initially reacted skeptically.

In the 1915 case United States v. Jin Fuey Moy, the Supreme Court halted the Treasury Department's attempt to criminalize citizens in possession of illicit drugs by a vote of seven to two. Just three years later (with two new members of the court) the justices heard the case Webb v. United States, which centered around the definition of "prescription." As mentioned before, the Harrison Act allowed anyone to obtain narcotics with a prescription written "in good faith." Following passage of the law, it was common practice for doctors to prescribe morphine for addicts—some did so to gradually wean patients off of drugs, others to maintain addictions without forcing addicts to turn to the black market. The Treasury Department decided to fight this practice.

In Webb, the Court decided (by a five to four vote) that prescriptions not written "in the course of professional treatment in the attempted *cure* of the [drug] habit" (emphasis added) were, in fact, not prescriptions, and doctors dispensing such prescriptions could be arrested and sent to prison (Webb v. U.S. at 99).

The final case in the series of opinions that turned the Drug War towards a punitive model came in 1922, when the Supreme Court decided (in United States v. Behrman) that any prescription issued to an addict whose only ailment was addiction itself, was illegal (Bertram, et al. 74-75). Thus the stage was finally set for the punishment-based drug policy that is the law of the land today.

The Modern Drug War

The creation of the War on Drugs as we know it today came during the Nixon Administration. President Richard Nixon sensed that an increased effort to end drug use would play well to his conservative supporters. In addition to new programs and funding, Nixon helped to reinforce the concept of drugs equaling crime, thus necessitating a punitive approach to all drug use and distribution (Bertram, et al. 105-06).

Presidents Ford and Carter continued the Drug War, but with a much lower profile. It was during the Reagan administration that the Drug War went into full tilt. But Reagan was not the only player who instigated the extreme measures that we live with today.

June, 1986, was the fateful month that University of Maryland basketball player Len Bias was drafted by the Boston Celtics. The day after the draft Bias died from the side effects of cocaine—his first time using the drug. This story rose to sensational proportions in the media, and the entire country had drugs on their minds when Congress went home for their Fourth of July recess. After Congress was back in session, the Speaker of the House, Tip O'Neill, called a meeting of House Democrats and announced that they needed to have a drug law reform bill ready in one month, before Congress adjourned for August recess ("Status of America's War on Drugs").

> "The drug war has done more to expand the predatory power of government at all levels than any other policy in the twentieth century, with the exception of the income tax."
>
> —David Kopel and Paul Blackman
> No More Wacos, page 326

Sheriff Bill Masters

Part of the reason O'Neill was so interested in this plan was that anti-drug rhetoric had worked very well for the Republicans in 1984, when they had won control of the Senate ("Sentencing"). The Legal Assistant to the House Judiciary Committee at the time, Eric Sterling, has remarked that the idea of drafting such major legislation (usually an 18-month process) in four weeks "was a horrifying prospect. We knew that mistakes were going to be made..." ("Status of America's War on Drugs").

One of the casualties of the rushed timetable was that there were no hearings. By the time mandatory minimums were inserted, there was no time to consult the DEA, Bureau of Prisons, the federal judiciary, or the Department of Justice. Once the mandatory minimums were inserted—giving a set sentence for a given amount of drugs—Senate Republicans decided that they would be "tougher" on the issue. Thus, they simultaneously increased sentence lengths and decreased the corresponding amounts in the mandatory minimum formulas. While all this hurried posturing was going on, there was no discussion of the fact that Congress had already imposed mandatory minimums in the 1950s but later repealed them because they had no effect on drug use ("Sentencing").

In a unique insight into the Congressional mindset, former Representative Dan Rostenkowski gave an interview in 1999 to talk about an encounter he had in prison. Rostenkowski was convicted of mail fraud and served time in the federal prison system after leaving the House. One day he met a young man who had received a seventeen-year sentence for a first-time offense for minor involvement in drug trafficking. Rostenkowski was shocked at the severity of the sentence, and then realized that he had voted for the bill which revised the sentencing guidelines. In a speech after his release from prison, he admitted that when he had cast his vote he was "swept along by the rhetoric about getting tough on crime." After his revelation in prison, however, Rostenkowski now views the new drug sentencing laws as "a sham" ("Sentencing").

It is important to note that most members of Congress rely on the word of the committees that examine legislation. Because of the political forces in play in 1986, the House Judiciary Committee hurriedly endorsed Tip O'Neill's plan and paved the way for our current prison population of more than two million.

Works Cited

Bertram, Eva, et al. Drug War Politics: The Price of Denial. Berkeley: U of California P, 1996.

Bogress, Brian. "Exporting United States drug law: An example of the international legal ramifications of the 'War on Drugs'." Brigham Young U of Law Review (1992) 165-191.

Musto, David. The American Disease: Origins of Narcotic Control. New Haven: Yale UP, 1973.

"Sentencing." This American Life. WBEZ/Public Radio International: October 22, 1999.

"Status of America's War on Drugs and the Effects on People on Both Sides of the Drug War." All Things Considered. Deborah Amos. National Public Radio. October 9, 2000.

United States. Department of Justice. Bureau of Justice Statistics

"Prisoners in 1999." By Allen Beck. Washington, DC: GPO, 2000.

United States v. Jin Fuey Moy. 241 U.S. 394. U.S. Supr. Ct. 1915. Webb v. United States. 249 U.S. 96. U.S. Supr. Ct. 1918.

Appendix C

Resources and Organizations

Sheriff Bill Masters

After Prohibition: An Adult Approach to Drug Policies in the 21st Century. Timothy Lynch, Ed. Cato Institute 2000. Roger Pilon and Steven Duke discuss the legal problems with the war on drugs. David B. Kopel of Colorado's Independence Institute writes of "Militarized Law Enforcement: The Drug War's Deadly Fruit." Ted Galen Carpenter describes more of the innocent victims of drug prohibition.

Why Our Drug Laws Have Failed and What We Can Do About It: A Judicial Indictment of the War on Drugs. Judge James P. Gray. Temple University Press, Philadelphia 2001. Judge Gray offers a detailed account of the history of drug prohibition and some useful advice for creating good policy. Particularly interesting are the comments Gray compiled from judges from around the nation who believe America's drug policy is on the wrong track.

Professor **Jeffrey A. Miron** of Boston University offers his papers about drug prohibition and violence at http://econ.bu.edu/miron.

Peter McWilliams, himself a victim of the drug war, lives on through his writings. His modern-day classic, *Ain't Nobody's Business If You Do*, is available on-line at http://mcwilliams.com.

For additional information about the innocent victims of the war on drugs, see the following books.

Lost Rights: The Destruction of American Liberty. James Bovard. St. Martin's Press 1994. Also see Bovard's **Freedom in Chains: The Rise of the State and the Demise of the Citizen**, St. Martin's Press 2000.

No More Wacos: What's Wrong with Federal Law Enforcement and How to Fix It. David B. Kopel and Paul H. Blackman. Prometheus Books 1997.

Send in the Waco Killers. Vin Suprynowicz. Mountain Media 1999.

Also, just published is **Human Rights and the US Drug War**, By Mikki Norris, Chris Conrad, Virginia Resner, Creative Xpressions 2001.

More of **Kopel's** work on drug and firearms policy is available at http://independenceinstitute.org. **Free-Market.net** publishes a wide range of issues papers, including one about drug prohibition at http://free-market.net/spotlight/drugs3.

DRCNet.org provides information about drug prohibition generally and about other law enforcement agents who oppose the drug war.

Common Sense for Drug Policy provides some information and links about the victims of the drug war at http://www.csdp.org/news/news/justcriminal.htm. Information specific to the death of Esequiel Hernandez is at http://www.dpft.org/hernandez/gallery.

The National Organization for the Reform of Marijuana Laws (NORML) hosts its page at http://www.norml.org. **The November Coalition**, which publishes *The Razor Wire*, is found at http://www.norml.org. **Families Against Mandatory Minimums** hosts its web page at http://famm.org. It includes stories of people locked up for years or even decades, taken from their families, for non-violent drug offenses.

The Cato Institute's web page contains many articles about drug prohibition; see http://cato.org/ and search for "drug" or "drug war." **The Libertarian Party** also provides information on the subject at www.lp.org. To search the web page of the **Future of Freedom Foundation**, see http://www.FFF.org. Articles from **Reason Magazine** are at http://www.reason.com.

In Colorado, the **Rocky Mountain Peace and Justice Center** is active in sentencing and drug policy reform. See http://www.rmpjc.org.

libertybill.net